Georg[es Bataille]

Georges B[ataille] ... thinkers of t[...] of life, Ba[...] examination[...] eroticism w[...] insight into [...] to it.

Largely [...] during the [...] and the U[...] post-structu[...]

Althoug[...] English, lit[...] available. T[...] a whole an[...] a difficult [...] readily wit[...] who does [...] seeks to d[...] critically examining the concepts he used.

The book will be of interest to both undergraduate and postgraduate students and is of particular value to anyone concerned with twentieth-century critical thought in France and the debate on post-modernism.

Michael Richardson is a writer and transla[tor ...] Bataille's *The Absence of Myth: Writings on [...]*

D1145815

Georges Bataille

Michael Richardson

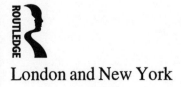

London and New York

First published 1994
by Routledge
11 New Fetter Lane, London EC4P 4EE

Simultaneously published in the USA and Canada
by Routledge
29 West 35th Street, New York, NY 10001

© 1994 Michael Richardson

Typeset in Times by LaserScript, Mitcham, Surrey
Printed and bound in Great Britain by
TJ Press (Padstow) Ltd, Padstow, Cornwall

British Library Cataloguing in Publication Data
A catalogue record for this book is available from the British Library

Library of Congress Cataloging in Publication Data has been applied for.

ISBN 0–415–09841–6   ISBN 0–415–09842–4 (pbk)

Contents

Preface

There's a marvellous moment in the film *Apocalypse Now* when Colonel Willard, as he travels up river to find Kurtz, ponders the information he receives about the man he will confront. As he studies photographs, documentary evidence and top secret files, as, in approaching the jungle stronghold, he more and more senses the presence of Kurtz, so at the same time his knowledge seems to slip away from him. He realises that the closer he gets to Kurtz, the more he finds out about him, the more he understands him, correspondingly the very process of understanding seems to undermine itself so that he feels in some way that paradoxically the more he knows the less he understands. It would be difficult to find a better illustration of one of the central paradoxes of the work of Georges Bataille, who was acutely aware of the slippage that knowledge brings in its wake. For Bataille knowledge had an inherent ability to undermine itself. He defined this as a dialectical relation between knowledge and non-knowledge.

To approach the thought of any major thinker is never a task to be treated lightly and in the case of Bataille this is made more acute because one needs to take into account his powerful analysis of the snares of knowledge. Bataille forces us to consider the extent to which our analysis may serve to reduce and domesticate the wildness of thought and so deprive it of the fascination appropriate to it. Unlike Willard, our given assignment is not assassination, but it can too easily become precisely that. Knowledge of any sort implies slippage and any worthwhile study of a book requires that one should try to establish a sense of affinity with the author. One of Bataille's favourite quotations from Nietzsche, to which he sought to remain true in his own work on the German thinker, expresses the difficulty of communication when faced with the thought of another. Nietzsche wrote: 'To be alone with a great thought is unbearable. I am seeking and calling to men to whom I can communicate this thought without their being destroyed by it.'[1]

Octavio Paz once wrote that it was impossible to write about André Breton other than in the language of passion. The same thing is true of Bataille, Breton's almost exact contemporary (in fact, he was one year younger than Breton and died four years before him), and to whom he presented a remarkable double image, a dark complement whose thought may be said to complete (in a dialectical sense) the ideas of the founder of surrealism.

Any study of Bataille can only be a quest marked by interpreting signs and traces. It is no use approaching his work with the aim of 'understanding' him in any conventional sense. Bataille refused in the most emphatic way any idea of absolute truth. His position assumed that if there was any truth at all it was that anything that claimed the status of truth was, by definition, false. Bataille therefore never wrote to convince but to provoke the reader, to draw the reader into his world and make him complicitous with his thought. He said: 'One mustn't read me: I don't want to be covered with evasions. I propose a challenge, not a book. I offer nothing for insomnia.'[2]

Against this background, one may wonder whether it is even legitimate to offer an introduction to Bataille's work. Despite the difficulties it raises, I feel it is important to do so. Bataille may have problematised the notion of knowledge and understanding, but he still believed there was a general truth to the universe that had to be sought out. If it was never possible to conceptualise this in any absolute form, if it constantly threatened to slip through our fingers, the quest itself nevertheless remained of the utmost importance. But one had to recognise that 'truth' lay not so much in knowledge itself but in the margin between knowledge and non-knowledge. If it was not something that could be grasped in concrete terms, this did not mean that truth did not exist, and we should be making a very serious error if we were to see what Bataille advances as providing any legitimation for the relativity of values and for the view that truth is therefore a chimera. The concept of understanding is not at all abandoned by the insistence of an interplay between knowledge and non-knowledge. In fact Bataille was keen to protect his work from misunderstanding. He did not present it to us in a disinterested spirit to allow us to make of it what we will. Quite the contrary, in fact: Bataille's concept of knowledge was always moral in nature. Without an appreciation of this moral framework, we are condemned to remain alien to Bataille's work. Since most of the commentary on Bataille in English has been poorly grounded, there therefore does seem to be a need for an introduction that tackles the context of his themes in their totality – and that is what this book strives to do. It is first of all essential to realise when approaching Bataille's work that before we can contemplate non-knowledge, we must first pass through knowledge. The former can never precede the latter.

With the upsurge of interest in Bataille it is also a little surprising that, although announced by a mass of translated work, this has been accompanied by few accessible critical studies. This work therefore endeavours to fill this gap. The aim is particularly to place Bataille's work in sociological perspective. Bataille's understanding of society and the relation of the individual to it is treated as central to his work.

The first chapter reviews the general issues raised by Bataille's work and looks at how it has been introduced into intellectual discourse. It particularly looks at the validity of claims that Bataille should be seen as a precursor of post-structuralism and post-modernism. A brief account of his life and work is given in Chapter 2, and Chapter 3 provides an introduction to the genealogy of his thought. It looks at the thinkers who had the most direct impact upon his own thinking and offers a preliminary explanation of the particular terminology he used.

Chapter 4 looks at social practice and methodological questions and Bataille's intellectual development and relation to orthodox scholarship. Bataille was unsatisfied with any scientific claims that worked only on the principle of making a thing of the object of study and put forward the notion of 'inner experience' as a necessary component within his own sociological investigation. This idea is examined in relation to Bataille's background, notably the importance of surrealism.

In Chapter 5 Bataille's notions of expenditure and the general economy are discussed in depth. Bataille offers a challenge to traditional economic theory based on the assumption of scarcity of resources. The problem, he insists, is the opposite and what we should be considering is how to use the excessive wealth that lies at our disposal. His sometimes unsatisfactory use of ethnographic data can serve to deflect argument about what is vital about his theories. His use of data is therefore held up to examination and though it is often found to be wanting it is argued that this does not bring into question what is vital about his overall argument.

Chapter 6 concentrates on death, communication and the experience of limits, considering Bataille's theory of eroticism and idea of taboo and transgression in the face of the awareness of death. This leads into a fuller discussion of the ideas behind inner experience and considers his understanding of myth, the sacred, sovereignty and reason.

Chapter 1

Introduction

Few stars have risen in the intellectual firmament as rapidly as that of Georges Bataille. When his *The Story of the Eye* was published in English translation in 1977,[1] few people would have imagined that within ten years its author would have become one of the most talked about thinkers of the age. That *The Story of the Eye* should have been published by Marion Boyers, a publisher specialising in important foreign-language authors with a restricted audience, seemed appropriate. In 1982, however, the story was reprinted in paperback by Penguin, something that offered a clear sign that a writer had 'arrived'. Since then translations of his work have come thick and fast.

At the time Bataille was little known except as a shadowy figure in French literature. For those who had a particular interest in surrealism he was a troubling presence on the margins of the French Surrealist Group, who had been treated harshly by André Breton in the *Second Manifesto of Surrealism* way back in 1929. Others knew him as an influence on post-structuralism, an *éminence grise* behind the ideas of thinkers like Foucault, Derrida, Baudrillard and Lyotard. But only a few specialists knew his work directly.

True, he had been translated before. His volumes on Manet and on prehistoric painting had been published in translation in 1955, the same year they appeared in French. However, this was probably due to their being published in a prestigious history of art series for which the publishers, Skira, doubtless had an arrangement whereby all the books would also be published in English translation. They were not, therefore, translated because of their intrinsic merits. His short text *Madame Edwarda* had also been published in 1955 by a small press specialising in erotica, Olympia Press. In 1962, the year of his death, his study *Eroticism* appeared, but despite its fashionable subject matter, it appears to have made little impact. In 1972, the novel *My Mother* was published, followed in 1973 by his study *Literature and Evil*. Neither book drew much interest and the former book sold only a tiny number of copies and was soon remaindered. Nothing suggested that there was any reason to believe that Bataille was of particular interest to an English language audience. In so far as it was recognised that his work was important, the prevailing view was that it related specifically to his own cultural context and that his focus on transgression and guilt – seen as residues of Catholicism – would have little appeal to an Anglo-Saxon audience. It is true that, with the exception of *Eroticism*, the importance of these books would be difficult to assess in isolation from the rest of his work, but even so it might have been thought that he was destined to remain a legendary figure on the margins of the margins of French literature whose thought would remain of interest only to specialists.

Besides, *The Story of the Eye*, despite being accompanied by essays by cultural luminaries Susan Sontag and Roland Barthes, was not the sort of work that could have been expected to generate interest among scholars and intellectuals, being, like *My Mother* and *Madame Edwarda*, a highly charged erotic, not to say pornographic and sacrilegious, story of sexual initiation. Given the general propensity in Anglo-Saxon countries to reduce discussion of sexuality to the discourse of moralistic titillation on the one hand or ideological correctness on the other, Bataille's single-minded examination of the violence of sexuality stands somewhat out on a limb. Also, the fact that *The Story of the Eye* was a book that Bataille never publicly acknowledged having written and which had only been published clandestinely under a pseudonym during his lifetime might also have been thought to discourage serious discussion.

If the erotic element may have helped to encourage sales of the book (although it did not seem to help *My Mother*), it does nothing to explain the peculiar appeal that Bataille's work has had during the past decade. In this time virtually all of Bataille's major texts have been translated into English (only *Methode de méditation* and a clutch of articles and conferences remain). Suddenly we find that a greater proportion of his work is available in English than that of his old adversaries like André Breton, Albert Camus or Jean-Paul Sartre. If this is not explained by the erotic qualities of the books, it is equally not due to their accessibility. Bataille can be a difficult writer and he does not make concessions to easy understanding, and this is further complicated by the range of Bataille's interests and the fact that he felt free to write about any topic that attracted him. There nevertheless remains a core to his thought that prevents this from ever degenerating into dilettantism, and today his importance is recognised in fields as diverse as philosophy, literature, theology, sociology, anthropology and even political economy.

What then are the reasons for this phenomenon? It is apparent that the rise of post-modernist criticism has been instrumental in encouraging the fashion for Bataille's work. He tends to be read through post-modernism and, with the popularity of thinkers like Derrida and Foucault, his work has thereby gained a sort of reflected prestige. But again, like the erotic element, this is only one factor of the way in which Bataille's thought has become of interest to a general readership and does not really explain why his work should have become as influential as it has. Indeed, despite its surface relation to ideas popularised by post-modernism, Bataille's thought fits uneasily into the supposed 'post-modern' condition. Even if it has been appropriated pell-mell into it, frequently his precepts have been reversed in the process and it is arguable that Bataille's appeal may have come about despite rather than because of the interests of post-modernism.

One key factor may have been that in an age dominated by cynical monetarist politics, people were in the mood to appreciate a thinker who had long scorned the whole principle of an economics of accumulation and utility to assert that the basis of economic health was a principle of pure exuberance. Bataille's idea of an unassimilable 'accursed share' that responded to a sense of the glorious loss and waste in an excessive expenditure may have been attractive.

Equally it may be that an age in which sexuality has come to be viewed as problematic in ways that had seemed irrelevant during the previous two decades may have caused people to be more attentive of the disturbing aspects of the sexual relation as explored by Bataille. While the advocates of the 'permissive society' would have found no comfort in Bataille's work, the incidence of Aids has brought a new sense of sexual insecurity. People have become acutely aware of the dangerous quality of sex and the resulting disquiet in sexual relations may respond in a direct way to the sense of anxiety that Bataille placed at the heart of his philosophy.

Whatever the reasons, though, Bataille is now firmly established as a key thinker of the age. Specialists may balk at Bataille's refusal to be tied to accepted boundaries of intellectual discourse and his insistence on focusing analysis within the widest possible horizon. Yet this also remains his strength. Even if his maverick way with social fact does sometimes lead to difficulties with his analysis, Bataille's whole ethos was based on a refusal to fragment the world up into tidy categories and he regarded it as pernicious to separate out any one factor or set of circumstances from the entire nexus of relations comprising any totality. He was not interested in playing safe and following well-charted routes. To do so was fraudulent. For this reason he felt it was not possible to contemplate philosophy without taking economic factors into account, nor the economy without considering the effusion of poetry. Such a project of totality is clearly unrealisable within the span of one person's life experience, and this is one of the 'impossible' paradoxes Bataille never flinches from in the way he approaches his material.

Since most of those who have been drawn to Bataille's work appear to have come to it through post-modernism, it is perhaps necessary to first of all examine the basis of his relation with the post-modernist surge, since fundamentally he is read 'through' Derrida, Kristeva, Sollers, Barthes, Lyotard, Foucault or Baudrillard,[2] all of whom have paid their tribute to the man many would like to sanctify as the prophet of deconstruction. I should say at the outset that I do not share this perception, which I believe is reductionist of the themes that Bataille wanted to tackle in his work.

My own interest in Bataille comes through a more general interest in surrealism and from an interest in the anthropological and philosophical issues his work raises. I first read *Eroticism* simultaneously with a reading of André Breton's *L'Amour fou* and was immediately struck by the correspondence between the two books, which seemed to me then – and with time this conviction has grown stronger – to complement and complete each other. Too often Breton and Bataille are presented as being antagonistic and their thought is contrasted to valorise one or the other. This ignores the respect that both men had for each other and which they expressed on numerous occasions over the years. It is this perceived antagonism that tends to be emphasised by writers associated with post-structuralism and this has served to give it undue prominence in debates centred on Bataille's work. For this reason the present work has a somewhat different perspective from most of the writings on Bataille in English.

While there are undoubtedly legitimate reasons for post-structuralism and post-modernism to see a pre-figuration of certain of their themes in Bataille's work, too often (and this is an ideological problem inherent in the post-modernist position in so far as it tends towards a contempt for the unfolding of history) it appropriates his work in a way that is contemptuous of its determinants. Whether or not one regards post-structuralism and post-modernism as fertile approaches towards cultural phenomenon in general, it must be problematic to append to its dominion a thinker who died before even structuralism had really become established as a specific methodological approach. In so far as the prefix post- is assumed so prevalently these days, it would seem that to take hold of a thinker who remained ignorant even of the advent of the ideology that one claimed to have superseded would seem to be distinctly problematic. Yet this problem rarely seems to be acknowledged.

In such circumstances, and especially if one is sceptical about the merits of the resultant focus established by the de-contextualisation of his work, it becomes particularly important to situate Bataille's work, and to make it clear that the post-modernist appropriation is not necessarily the only legitimate perspective in which it can be viewed. Let us then examine how some of those writers connected with post-modernism have approached Bataille's work.

Of those thinkers mentioned above, whose names are frequently invoked in relation to Bataille, only Jean Baudrillard seems to have any real understanding of, or feel for, the centrality of Bataille's work. Certainly in his early work Baudrillard did draw on concepts that he derived from Bataille. This is especially the case with *L'Échange symbolique de la mort*, and he does engage with Bataille's ideas in a way that promises much. But this soon starts to deviate in a direction that serves to invert Bataille's concepts.

Bataille continues to be an influence, but the approach Baudrillard then adopts serves to vulgarise Bataille, since it draws only on the most negative aspects of his thought. What Baudrillard dispenses with (which was essential for Bataille) is any notion of moral centring. Everything becomes a swirl of negative possibilities: there is nothing to choose since nothing has legitimacy, there are no underlying structures to reality (which dissolves into hyper-reality), there is no possibility of social solidarity or participation. Meaning goes out of the window in a helpless surrender not to darkness but to exasperation. Where Bataille wanted to give an unqualified 'yes' to the universe, Baudrillard gives an equally unqualified 'no' to it. In the end this negative response serves to dissolve negation, since it offers no positive against which negation can be measured and so becomes a mere floating critique that finally only operates as a parody of itself. From this perspective, Baudrillard merely turned Bataille on his head and in the process the critique that Baudrillard has developed serves as nothing but a burlesque simulation of the issues Bataille was concerned with.

Many of the other writers mentioned appear to have only a passing acquaintance with Bataille's work and reading what they have written one has the feeling that, far from having influenced them, most of them only considered his writing because it was fashionable to do so rather than from a genuine interest in the questions it tackles.

An exception must be made for Foucault, who was undoubtedly influenced by Bataille in many ways. However, whether he really understood Bataille's work in any meaningful way is seriously open to doubt, since Foucault's way of thinking seems completely alien to that of Bataille and in great part his approach is incommensurate with Bataille's. The article he wrote on Bataille's death,[3] even if it has interest in its own right in regard to Foucault's own concerns, in so far as it deals with Bataille the best that can be said about it is that it takes misunderstanding to its limit as it utilises Bataille's concepts for purposes that correspond with nothing at all in Bataille's own work. In this article Foucault treats transgression in a way that could hardly be further from Bataille's own approach. First, he isolates it as a thing in itself, abstracting it from its relation with taboo, something without which, in Bataille's view, it had no meaning. Cast adrift in this way, Bataille's very concrete notion of transgression is completely undermined. For Foucault transgression has meaning in itself as a particular sensibility. He describes what for Bataille was the common experience of all mankind as 'a singular experience'.[4] For Foucault transgression is a crucial element of contemporary society whereas Bataille believed it was being systematically excluded and that it was impossible for transgression to be anything but impotence within the society in which we live.

When Foucault deals with other questions of concern to Bataille – like sexuality or the growth of individualism – the frame of reference he establishes for his study is just as alien to Bataille's own understanding. It is not so much that one can say that Foucault is in disagreement with Bataille, but that what interests him belongs to a different discourse. This is in great part explained by the fact that they came from different generations. Foucault in a sense was in revolt against the tradition to which Bataille belonged, and to fit Bataille to what Foucault wanted him to be requires a fundamental distortion of Bataille's thought. By claiming not only Bataille, but also Roussel and Artaud, Foucault asserts a continuity in French thought that does not exist.

In reaction to Hegel, whose philosophy had dominated French intellectual life from 1930 to 1950,[5] Foucault returned to a neo-Kantian framework as the basis for his social critique. Bataille's relation with Hegel is complex and he certainly felt ambivalent about elements in Hegelian philosophy, but he was still of a generation that came to Hegel with a sense of wonder and recognition and his thinking is fully within the frame of dialectical reasoning. It would have been impossible for him to reject Hegel as Foucault did.

This is especially so in that what Foucault reacted against most of all was the Hegelian dialectic, and especially against the dialectic of master and slave. This was exactly where Bataille was most clearly in accord with Hegel. Foucault's pluralistic viewpoint was offended by the relation Hegel drew between master and slave, which makes the sort of power relation Foucault thought existed between people inconceivable. Foucault could not see how people could be bound in such a complicitous way and therefore he believed that to make a relation between master and slave was simply a fiction and thus of little analytical value. From the same perspective, Foucault considers that concepts like 'individual' or 'society' are equally fictive. In Foucault there is no fixity. Every concept is defined through its discursive reference. This is manifestly against the centrality of Bataille's thought and can even be said to be fundamentally anti-Bataillean. For Bataille to establish the reality of every concept was a fundamental methodological necessity. And for Bataille it was Hegel's great achievement, with the notion of the master and slave relation, to have conceptualised a fundamental reality lying within human consciousness. This was a real relation for Bataille, not a discursive concept. Discourse was a snare that had to be avoided. With the notion of discourse he established, Foucault takes a starting point that Bataille insisted was invalid – the idea that discursive structures serve their own interests and impose themselves against individual specificity. Everything in Foucault revolves around ideas of power and knowledge refused by Bataille. For Bataille we *are* society. Therefore concepts like power and knowledge can never take form isolated from the totality of the societal relations which found them. For Bataille power and knowledge are dynamic concepts inherent in human activity and having no meaning in themselves. They cannot be abstracted in the way Foucault did. It is societal interaction that defines what we are as individuals and this implies an inextricable link that can never be broken. Power does not exist in the abstract, as it does in Foucault's analysis. The essence of Hegel's master and slave relation is complicity: the reality of the slave is the master, the reality of the master the slave. In this perspective, individuals can never be imposed upon. If they are subject to oppression it is because they are complicitous with the power relation placed above them. In the same way the power relation can be broken through a withdrawal of such complicity. Society, it should be understood, is for Bataille an organic whole that includes the individual; it too is not at all a discursive concept.

For Foucault, too, what is important is the plurality of being. He refused totality, which he saw as related to power relations. Bataille had exactly the opposite viewpoint, considering that the desire to cut things up into segments (we might say into separate discourses) was a way of avoiding the essential questions the material raised. The crucial difference between the two men is contained in this quotation by Foucault: 'What reason perceives as *its* necessity, or rather, what different forms of rationality offer as their necessary being, can perfectly well be shown to have a history; and the network of contingencies from which it emerges can be traced . . . since these things have been made, they can be unmade, as long as we know how it was that they were made.'[6] While the objective target of this statement is rationality, also implicit in it is an undermining of dialectical reasoning. Foucault breaks up reason into different forms of rationality whose contingency in the process becomes clear (by virtue of the fact that they have been separated out). Although Bataille would agree that rationality has extremely complex ideological implications, the idea that it lacked necessity would have been incomprehensible to Bataille, while the latter proposition would be unacceptable, since Bataille's whole approach is manifestly based in the impossibility of understanding any network of contingencies from such a perspective. He would also refuse both to deny the vital quality of such contingencies and to accept the proposition that such 'things' could be 'made'. For Bataille the nexus of social relations is established through a to-and-fro movement that is fundamentally unknowable (because it stands outside the concept of understanding) and certainly there could never be any possibility of 're-making' it. It was transformation, not deconstruction, that was the focus for change in Bataille's view. There is at work here a radically different concept of the way in which phenomena respond to each other such as makes it difficult to even discuss Bataille's work in relation to that of Foucault. Their starting-points are just so different.

Both Baudrillard and Foucault are drawn to Bataille because of what they see as a methodological justification for non-systematic thinking and a downplaying of the need to justify an argument with empirical proof. However, both ignore the fact that Bataille did not at all deny the validity of empirically-based and systematic thought. He pointed out rather its limits and the fact that it could not consider itself complete without engaging with its complementary need for non-knowledge. Since both Foucault and Baudrillard equally ignore the consequences of non-knowledge, they are not really entitled to draw any support for their own concepts of the structure of knowledge from Bataille.

For this reason, while it may be that his understanding of Bataille provides Foucault with fertile ground upon which to base his own thinking, then (while this influence is relevant to a study of Foucault's own work), to see Bataille's work through Foucault (or any other thinker who came after him) is to decontextualise it and distort, if not destroy, his essential arguments.

Does it matter that Bataille's work has often been taken in a direction he would not have recognised? Even if post-modernism has misrepresented Bataille has it not made his thought relevant to the present day? That it does matter is shown clearly if one reads the lecture that Habermas devotes to Bataille in *The Philosophical Discourse of Modernity*.[7] As perceptive as this study is, Habermas nevertheless completely mis-understands Bataille's argument, which he seems to consider to be essentially a critique of reason. Later in this book we will examine the issues raised by Habermas's contentions, but we should note here that Bataille certainly never saw his work as representing a *critique* of reason. Habermas could only have made this error because he was reading Bataille within the context of post-modernism.

It also important to emphasise Bataille's distance from post-modernism for other reasons. First, because post-modernism reasserts textual authority through a discourse of incompletion. Where Bataille was suspicious of writing and sought to elude the frame of discourse as far as possible, post-modernists have considered his texts expressly as an engagement with discourse. In so doing they have effectively cut the lifeblood away from his thought. The idea that reality is merely textual is quite alien to Bataille, who believed that the basis of thought particularly lay in analogy, the very basis of which is denied by a post-modernism that refuses to privilege any particular representation. This means, for instance, that transgression, for Bataille a dynamic motion that determines the nature of society, is deprived of this very dynamism and becomes a quantitative accumulation to challenge the taboo for supremacy (this is post-modernist understanding of 'subversion'). For Bataille the play between taboo and transgression was a complex moral relation in which neither has any privileged status *vis-à-vis* the other. Transgression does not 'subvert' the taboo: it completes and reinforces it.

This means that there is a gulf between Bataille's conception of the nature of reality and that put forward by post-modernism. Since thinking can be both analogical and conceptual for Bataille, its meaning is as much to be found in its margins as within the manifestation itself. By giving primacy to concepts like textuality, discourse or simulation, post-modernism displaces reality and denies the possibility of meaning lying in the margins. Its procedure is to accept the basis of conceptual thought but try to undermine it. It no more leaves a space for analogical thought than does rationalism.

Equally, where Bataille desired the disintegration of the subject and protested against the tyranny of the individual, in post-modernism the subject is disintegrated as a means of gaining access to a plurality of discourse. In so far as Bataille is invoked in this argument, we see his concepts being used to obscure the precision of his thought. To the extent that we can identify the core element of the post-modernist attitude, we might say that it was tied towards a belief in the autonomy of textual authority, asserting that texts have an existence that is independent of their referents and can be discussed from such a perspective. This is what connects up Foucault's notion of 'discourse', Derrida's notion of 'text' and Baudrillard's of 'simulation'. If we accept this perspective, I suppose one can argue that it is of no consequence how Bataille's thought is interpreted since what he wrote is not extricably linked with a man who once lived and was named Georges Bataille, but rather comes to mean what we want it to mean. Even if we accept the validity of this argument, though, we must also recognise that it is fundamentally at odds with Bataille's own perspective, since he considered textual authority to be a very feeble thing having little vitality in itself. To undermine it is not too difficult, but serves little purpose.

Post-modernism, too, emerges from a historical context overwhelmed in disillusion and a loss of hope in the possibilities of revolutionary change, possibilities that seem to have been extinguished in the void that has followed the euphoria of 1968. Bataille's philosophy, which refuses to offer any hope, is therefore highly attractive. However, those drawn to Bataille for this reason ignore the fact that Bataille's lack of hope arises from his own existential sensibility. It is not a response to a sense of disillusion. Bataille's position is to refuse any possibility of hope, to accept whatever life may offer and not strive to realise any ideal. If Bataille was drawn to communism, it was not out of any belief that communism offered solutions to the human condition, but primarily because he saw communism as inevitable given the perverse and unsustainable ideological precepts upon which capitalism was based. For him communism was desirable, but it contained no seeds of hope. For Bataille there was no such solution to the human condition. But if Bataille refuses hope, he equally refuses to accept hopelessness and a collapse into cynicism. He had a clear sense of human destiny and never succumbed to despair or despondency: at root his work is profoundly affirmative of the experience of being alive.

Bataille belonged to a revolutionary era. If he was a revolutionary thinker, it was as part of the movement of his time.

Such an era cannot be understood in terms of our present age, which no one would deny is highly conventional and devoid of the imagination to contemplate any transformation of society. No one today has the slightest belief in the revolution that Bataille, right to the end of his life, believed to be imminent. The gulf separating us from the issues that were of vital importance to intellectuals of Bataille's generation is thus a vast one.

It is often strange that in intellectual discourse we tend to accept a cutting short of chronological distance that is never permitted in spatial distance. Where the first rule of an ethnologist is to understand a different society in its own terms and not appropriate it to our own values, when we consider events occurring in a different time within our own culture we have a tendency to assume that the frame of reference remains the same. This is something that post-modernism, in underlining textual and discursive authority, has accentuated. It is a problem that is particularly acute in relation to Bataille, because his work has become known in English through the claims that others have made on his behalf a long time after he had finished writing. Irrespective of the ideological postulates of post-modernism, this would serve as a distorting screen and would necessitate that we try to look beyond what has been written since his time to the background of his own work rather than to that of those who came after. But further than this, the fact is that for all its claims to encourage a plurality of discourse, the ideology of post-modernism has served to set an extremely narrow agenda, often in an authoritarian way. In this sense it reveals its roots, which lie in French Communist Party discourse of the fifties, whose totalitarian impulse it retains even if it reacts against any imposition of the dogmatic precepts of 'scientific Marxism' based on historical materialism. Nevertheless, in relation to Stalinist dogma post-modernism tends to merely reverse the frame of reference so that it becomes the lack of historical structure that is just as dogmatically asserted.

To appreciate what is important about Bataille's work it is crucial to consider him within the context of his own period, not to appropriate him to ours. To see him through Foucault, Derrida or Baudrillard is to emasculate what is original in his work.

For critics emerging from post-modernism, one of the attractive features of Bataille's work is its unsystematic nature and the fact that he appears to eschew the usual standards of evidence to put forward propositions whose audaciousness is directly connected to this lack of system or project. This is viewed as something essential to Bataille's thought. It represents what is radical about him, so enabling him to escape the snares of discourse and gain a freewheeling quality that stands above power relations. One cannot write about Bataille for this reason, because Bataille's thought is not about anything: it is a discourse that only obeys its own requirements. Such nominalism would certainly have disconcerted Bataille and we have already raised doubts about the real applicability of this argument to his thought. Denis Hollier, whose *La Prise de la concorde* (translated as *Beyond Architecture*) has been of central importance in establishing this point of view, denies that it is valid to write a book *about* Bataille, stating that his own intent has been specifically not to write a book that would be *about* Bataille:

> So. Is this to be a study on Bataille? or over him? or above him? . . . Writing on is the epitome of a discourse in control, calmly assured of its position. It is deployed with calm assurance in a realm over which it has taken possession, and it has inventoried after first closing it off, to make sure it is absolutely safe. This discourse runs no risk at all: it is not uneasy about the future, it steadily expands . . .[8]

This statement is presented with no qualification and reduces all discourse (except of course its own) to the same level, so providing an ideological justification for the writer to say what he likes without any qualification. He continues: 'To write *on* Bataille is . . . to betray him. At the same time to miss him. To write *on* Bataille is not to *write* on Bataille.'[9] Perhaps there might be something in this, but if so, one wonders why Hollier invokes Bataille's name at all in *La Prise de la concorde*. Since the argument developed in Hollier's book essentially concerns the deleterious effects of architectural principles and the unhealthy effects of building or planning for the future, why does he not simply establish his argument and allow it to stand on its own premises? Why does he need Bataille? It is true that this is one element of Bataille's thought, but for Bataille it rests on complex postulates ignored by Hollier. The issue raised by Hollier, though, remains straightforward. And so, whose is the argument that is developed in *La Prise de la concorde*? Is it Bataille's or is it Hollier's? If the former, then the book is *about* Bataille in exactly the way Hollier condemns. If it is Hollier's then he is manipulating Bataille's thought for his own purposes. In actual fact, its every sentence draws on his authority. It uses this authority to simultaneously legitimate itself and to absolve itself from any charge of distortion or misinterpretation. There is a disingenuousness of thought here that uses subterfuge to exonerate itself and reduce thought even as it claims to open it up. By means of a vast store of erudite ignorance, Hollier assumes the authority to tell us how to think.

In itself the approach he advocates is not illegitimate, providing it is made clear that it is a personal approach. But to put it forward as an ideological principle and to assert that consideration of Bataille's work in any other way is unacceptable, to condemn it out of hand as a 'betrayal', is an example of crass ignorance and intolerance.

It is true that to some degree one does betray Bataille by writing about him, since inevitably this brings his thought into the realm of discourse, something which inevitably destroys it. But this is one of the paradoxes at the heart of Bataille's work, paradoxes of which he was fully aware and which are central to its understanding. All communication involves loss, but this is the price that has to be paid for someone who *needs* to communicate. It is a necessity that cannot be avoided. By writing his books, Bataille was betraying himself. But by not writing them, he would have been committing an even graver betrayal, since he would have failed to have responded to the necessity that gave rise to his writing them. Any writer is faced with the same dilemma if he accepts the terms of reference Bataille puts forward, no matter what the subject, and Bataille would certainly not say that this was something only of relevance to his own work: for him to write about any writer is in a sense a betrayal. One doesn't escape the dilemma by stating that a book that invokes Bataille's name and discusses his thought, is not 'about' him.

It also seems particularly inappropriate to make this point about a writer who established a journal, *Critique*, which concentrated exclusively on studies *about* particular books. Equally, in his own work Bataille went to great pains to protect the thought of Nietzsche from what he considered misinterpretations, not only from the charge of fascism, but also from contentions about his work advanced in important books by André Gide and Thomas Mann.[10] Bataille indeed frequently complains about all the misinterpretations foisted upon Nietzsche in an often cavalier manner and contends that 'even since he became famous has he ever been anything but an occasion for misunderstanding?'[11] We might wonder if this insight was not perhaps prescient of Bataille's own fate.

There can be little doubt that for Bataille there was an inherent truth to a writer's work which, far from being of no consequence, mattered very much. 'As long as I misunderstand things,' he wrote, 'my claim to un-knowing is an empty one.'[12] It therefore seems highly unlikely that Bataille would have approved of a book written vaguely 'around' his thought, especially as in his book Hollier presents Bataille rather like an insufferable brat on holiday who gets his pleasure from kicking down the other kid's sand castles. Such reductionism is the last thing Bataille's work deserves. For him to write was a necessary and onerous task. The condition of life should be silence. One needed a good reason to break that silence. Nothing was more foreign to his temperament than the 'pleasure of the text' so beloved by post-modernists. For Bataille a great responsibility attached to writers, which should never be taken lightly: one should never write unless compelled to do so. To assert, as Hollier seems to do, that intellectual discourse, in so far as Bataille conceived it, acted through a sort of interminable chain letter passing from one person to another to eternity trivialises the necessity that Bataille perceived in his own work. He would have been appalled by the idea of some endless discourse that lacked any moral centring.

It may be that Bataille's book *On Nietzsche*, would not satisfy a Nietzsche scholar. In this book, it is true that Bataille sought to examine Nietzsche's thought not in the narrow way of the specialist, but to engage in a sort of communication with it. But, at the same time, it would be false to say that Bataille wrote this book in a spirit of antagonism to recognised Nietzsche scholarship. Quite the contrary: he is very much indebted to such scholarship, which he would have been the last to undermine. *On Nietzsche* is rather an exploration of Nietzsche's thought in relation to Bataille's own concerns. He does not use Nietzsche in order to found his own authority, and the book necessarily tells us far more about Bataille than about Nietzsche. He certainly did not write in the unsystematic way he did in order to outwit discourse, but because it was the only appropriate way to explore the realms of inner experience and the general economy, which were not reducible to orthodox research methods.

Hollier, on the other hand, appropriates Bataille's approach for the benefit of ordinary academic discourse, serving in the process to conflate scholarship with interpretation so as to hypocritically give authority to his account. We need to see beyond this manoeuvre. Bataille's book on Nietzsche is not a book to be recommended if one wants to know anything about Nietzsche. It is a work we read if we want to know about Bataille. Perhaps the same criterion should be applied to Hollier's book, for there is no question that it tells us more about Hollier than it does about Bataille.

To understand Bataille's position we therefore need to take into account the context in which he developed and came to write his books. Above all, he was formed in a generation that came of age during the First World War, a generation that saw the birth of surrealism, a movement that can be said effectively to frame Bataille's thought, even if to some degree his relation with it is problematic.

Despite what has sometimes been suggested, Bataille was not a grand solitary at odds with the intellectual currents of his time who, because of this, anticipated the later post-modernism. Bataille's concerns are fully explicable within the inter-war period in which he is by no means an out-of-place figure. Like most other writers connected with the surrealist movement, Bataille does not write to establish the usual one-to-one relation with the reader. He does not write to convince and does not expect the reader to passively accept his 'message'. He has no time for inductive learning. Rather he speaks in a tone of intimacy and desires a confidence and complicity with the reader. His writing is a provocation. It sets traps for the unwary, and seeks to jolt the passive reader out of complacency. In order to understand Bataille it is necessary to meet the challenge he lays down and enter into the intimate domain he wanted to establish. Nothing he wrote can be accepted purely at face value: Bataille was touched with a mischievous fondness to dissemble, to leave a false trace. This does not mean that he sought to deceive but rather that, again like most of the surrealists, he writes in the way of the alchemists of old, eager to withhold as much as they reveal as they try to take the reader on their own journey of discovery. It is not possible to read his work in a conventional way; one needs to interrogate it, ask questions of it, take it into oneself and apply it through one's own experience.

Bataille can be a lucid thinker, but can also be obscure. But the extent to which his work is difficult is due to the fact that he is often 'thinking out loud' and if the meaning of a passage appears obscure to us then it is because it was in all likelihood equally obscure to Bataille himself. When he defined the way he thought as being like 'a girl taking off her dress' he also defined the way he wrote.

Nevertheless, to assume from this that because Bataille's approach was unorthodox and provocative it was therefore aimed at the subversion of intellectual discourse is a proposition to be treated with some caution. Despite considering excess as a path of enlightenment, Bataille remained a discreet writer. He liked silence and never sought the limelight, which disconcerted him. He was recently described by J.G. Merquior as being 'an incendiary in slippers'.[13] This was meant to be an insult, but one feels that the designation would not have displeased Bataille, who was always keen to maintain a distance from a vehement verbalism.

Bataille never held a university post, and never appears to have sought one. But his reason was not that he despised disciplined scholarly work. Again like all those connected with surrealism at this time, he believed that the professionalism of university of life mitigated against intellectual inquiry and made especially difficult the sort of activist and interested knowledge he wanted to pursue. During the inter-war years not one of those surrealists particularly interested in intellectual questions (and we can particularly here cite Jules Monnerot, Roger Caillois, Pierre Mabille, Nicolas Calas, Pierre Naville) ever held an academic post. Bataille saw himself in the line of nineteenth-century outsiders like Marx, Kierkegaard, Nietzsche and even Comte, the vitality of whose thought he believed was conditioned by the fact that they remained outside the confines of an academic career properly speaking. For Bataille, a sense of risk and an independence from the *requirement to think* imposed by an educational establishment were essential pre-requisites for the freedom of thought. He believed that distance is always a necessary criterion for intellectual enquiry if we wish to touch the essentiality of being:

> It is through an intimate cessation of all "intellectual operations" that the mind is laid bare. If not, *discourse* maintains it in its little complacency. Discourse, if it wishes to, can blow like a gale wind – whatever effort I make, the wind cannot chill by the fireside. The difference between inner experience and philosophy resides principally in this: that in experience, what is stated is nothing, if not a means and even, as much as a means, an obstacle; what counts is no longer the statement of the wind, but the wind.[14]

Given this, it seems rather ironic that most of his post-modernist admirers advance their 'deconstruction' from within secure university posts, quite content to sit in front of the academic fireside and play games with the statement of the wind rather than confront the wind itself.

For Bataille life is paradoxical and his sociology reflects this paradox, being based on an impossible conjunction between states of being that are inherent to our nature as human beings. Living with a realisation of our own impermanence and with the fact that ultimately we shall die, we turn our back on this awareness and try to live our lives as if they took place in an eternal duration. We build and plan for a future that will never come, and which we do not really desire since our whole being is tied to a temporal reality that would find any trans-cendant relation with a beyond unsatisfactory. Correlatively, we place belief in just such a transcendence as a way to escape being in the world. Bataille tried to confront this reality head-on and without making concessions. He asked: how do we live with the realisation of our own deaths? Equally he denied all possibility of ultimate knowledge or of our ever fully understanding the world: life was by definition a state of incompletion. It was even a sickness to try to discover it since, 'the world never offers simple moments, it never corresponds to any situation I might describe, but rather to the imbroglio of relations that arise from the continual opposition of the most diverse possibilities.'[15]

Given the immediacy of this demand, should one not allow Bataille's work to stand for itself, leave it in grand isolation, so that each of his readers will come to it afresh and make of it what they will? If this was possible, the results might be interesting, but the fact is that any reader comes with their own pre-conceptions and it is never possible to approach any work entirely afresh. The labyrinth was an image that had particular importance for Bataille, and his own work can present the aspect of being a complex labyrinth itself, with many dead ends and hiatuses, with traps and false beginnings. In this respect it reflects the materiality of Bataille's conception of reality. For the labyrinth is not simply existence itself but also the human body. In so far as Bataille's writing can be seen to be an emanation of the body, this labyrinthine quality is a mark of its authenticity. But who would dare enter the labyrinth without anything to guide them? To do so would be to risk wandering around aimlessly in sullen incomprehension, unable, so to speak, to see the wood for the trees, or rather mistaking each dead end for a world. The hope of this book is therefore to provide an a preliminary investigation of the labyrinth of Bataille's thinking without exhausting its mysteries.

Chapter 2

Life and context of work

According to what Bataille tells us he had a terrible childhood. He was born from peasant stock on 10 September 1897 at Billon, Puy-de-Dome, in central France (some ten miles from Clermont-Ferrant). His father was blind and syphilitic and, when Bataille was three, suffered a general paralysis. Soon afterwards the family moved to Rheims. His school had other notable pupils: before Bataille there had been the poet Paul Fort, and, a few years later, fellow surrealist marginals, Roger Caillois, René Daumal and Roger Gilbert-Lecomte would also pass through its gates. He tells us he was a lazy and insolent child, but after starting his baccalaureate suddenly changed and became a model student. At the same time, as an act of rebellion against his parents lack of interest in religion, he converted to Catholicism. With the coming of war in 1914 he was evacuated, together with his mother, since Rheims was subject to German bombardment, leaving behind his father, who was to die in the city in 1916. He was called up to fight in the army, but was soon demobilised on the grounds of ill health following a bout of tuberculosis.

Bataille defined his period:

> I belong to a turbulent generation, born to literary life in the tumult of surrealism. In the years after the Great War there was a feeling which was about to overflow. Literature was stifling within its limitations and seemed pregnant with revolution.[1]

Unlike most of the other surrealists, though, this turbulence seems to have affected Bataille on the rebound. For most of the first generation surrealists the First World War determined that revolt. Theirs was a sense of disgust at a loss and devastation in the service of a cause that no one could support. For most of those who came to surrealism it was impossible not to hate a society and a culture responsible for such carnage.

Bataille's own experience of the war was more discreet. At this time, he tells us (and everything we know bears this out), he was a pious and diligent young man. His first surviving writing confirms this impression. In 1919 he published a short text called 'Notre-Dame de Rheims', in which he laments the bombing of the cathedral in the war and prays for its restoration. It is not the sort of text we might expect from someone who would later be drawn into the boiling cauldron of left-wing surrealist circles. The impression given is more that of the sort of young man who would soon be drawn towards the neo-fascism of 'L'Action Française'.

However, politics seem to have played no part in this moment of his life. In 1917 he had joined the seminary of Saint-Fleur with the intention of becoming a priest or a monk. Three years later, he tells us, he lost his faith and his vocation during a stay at a Benedictine monastery in the Isle of Wight because 'his Catholicism caused a woman he loved to shed tears'.[2] He nevertheless remained a good student at the École des Chartres, poring over medieval texts and submitting his thesis on 'The Order of Chivalry, told in verse from the thirteenth century' at the beginning of 1922.

The following month he obtained a fellowship at the School of Advanced Hispanic Studies in Madrid. From here he travelled extensively around Southern Spain and dreamed of far-away travel: Morocco, Russia, China and especially Tibet. He began an intensive study of foreign languages, including Russian and Tibetan, but soon lost interest in the idea. Nevertheless, two other events of 1922 had a decisive impact on him, and in many ways determined the course of his life. In May he witnessed the death of the bullfighter Manuelo Granero, whose skull was split open by the horns of a bull at the Madrid bullfight and, later in the year, he began to read Nietzsche.

By the end of 1922, he had obtained a position at the Bibliothèque Nationale in Paris. He then threw himself into philosophy with the same gusto he had previously displayed for religion and medieval studies. Becoming a pupil of Leon Chestov, he immersed himself in readings of Dostoyevsky, Kierkegaard, Pascal and especially Nietzsche.

He was also drawn by the attractions of dissolution and his diligence in exploring Parisian night-life was no less apparent as he assiduously frequented bordellos whilst also making himself known in intellectual circles. Apparently finding Dadaism 'not idiotic enough', since its 'no' was too conventional, he advocated a movement which would say 'yes' to everything. At the same time, through friendships with Michel Leiris, André Masson and Theodore Fraenkel he became drawn into the surrealist circle, but found the atmosphere intimidating and maintained a distance.

The violent swings of his personality are revealed in his earliest writings. He destroyed a text called 'W.C.', which he says was 'violently opposed to all dignity'. But other texts like 'The Solar Anus' and 'The Pineal Eye' bear witness to his disturbed state, which caused him to seek treatment with the psychoanalyst Adrian Borel. He says that 'the psychoanalysis has a decisive result; by August 1927 it put an end to the series of dreary mishaps and failures in which he had been floundering, but not to the state of intellectual intensity, which still persists.'[3]

At this time he is publishing his first scholarly texts in a high-class art and archaeology journal called *Aréthuse*. In 1927, too, his political instincts were aroused by the demonstrations in favour of Sacco and Vanzetti, in which he participated.

In 1928 he married Silvia Maklès, a young actress who would later make a name for herself in films by Renoir, Carné and other leading directors (she is seen most radiantly in Renoir's *Une partie de compagne* (1936), in which Bataille also had a small part as a country priest). Their daughter, Laurence, would be born in 1930. Bataille also published his first novel, *The Story of the Eye*, clandestinely under the pseudonym 'Lord Auch'. In April the journal *Documents* was founded by the art collector Georges Wildenstein and Bataille was appointed secretary-general. In the following months he will write numerous articles for the review and take an ever-greater editorial role until he becomes the *de facto* editor in collaboration with his friend Georges-Henri Rivière, director of the ethnographic Musée du Trocadéro. As the Surrealist Group falls apart in the later part of 1929, Bataille gathers around him most of the dissidents, who publish in the journal. Rightly or wrongly, André Breton sees this as an attempt to found a counter-Surrealist Group and the *Second Manifesto of Surrealism* contains insults against many of his former friends, reserving a special place for a venomous attack on Bataille. Seizing on the articles Bataille has written in *Documents*, Breton accuses him of being a 'vulgar materialist' and an 'obsessive'. Bataille gathers the dissidents for an equally violent attack on Breton, the collective pamphlet *Un cadavre*, in which, trading insults, Bataille calls Breton a 'religious windbag' and a 'neutered lion'.

Documents ceased publication in 1931. In the meantime, Bataille's thinking had been considerably widened by attending the lectures of Marcel Mauss on anthropology and politically deepened by readings of Hegel, Sade, Marx, Trotsky and Stirner. He had also become more politically involved, joining Boris Souvarine's 'Cercle Communiste Démocratique' along with surrealist dissidents Leiris, Queneau, Baron, Morise and Tual. He also took part in an abortive attempt to found a 'popular university', Masses, and published his first important articles, 'The notion of expenditure' and 'The psychological structure of fascism'.

In 1934, two further decisive encounters take place: he attends the lectures of Alexandre Kojève at the École des Hautes Études. His marriage breaks up (Sylvia will later marry Jacques Lacan) and he meets Colette Peignot, with whom he is to have an intense and violent relationship and whose death in 1938 will have a devastating effect upon his life.

In 1935 he established, on the initiative of Roger Caillois and in collaboration with André Breton and the surrealists (with whom he had become reconciled), an anti-popular-front political group called 'Contre-attaque', which had for its aim the re-establishment of revolutionary principles betrayed by the Communist and Socialist Parties. Following its collapse in 1936, he created the College of Sociology, a group that will have for its aim an 'activist sociology', as well as the mysterious 'Acéphale', a secret society that represented a 'voyage out of this world'. In 1938, too, he tried to set up a 'Society for Collective Psychology' with the psychoanalysts Adrian Borel and René Allendy.

The coming of the war brought an end to both of these groups and Bataille withdrew into himself, turning to yoga and beginning to write his most introspective books, *Le Coupable* and *L'Expérience intérieure* in addition to the intense erotic tales *Madame Edwarda* and *The Dead Man*. His recurrent tuberculosis leads to his leaving the Bibliothèque Nationale in 1942 and he retired to Vézeley in the French countryside to recuperate. *L'Expérience intérieure* is published in 1943, and in the next few years he immersed himself in a number of projects, which range from the poems of *L'Archangélique* to the reflections of *Sur Nietzsche* and the 'economic' analysis of *La Part maudite*.

In 1946 he founded a new journal, *Critique*, which was to become one of the most respected of French scholarly journals (and is still being published today).

The same year he marries for the second time: to Diane de Beauharnais, and their daughter Julie will be born in 1948. In 1947 he began to give guest lectures at the Collège Philosophique and edited a series of books for the publishers Minuit, but remained unemployed and was in severe financial difficulties until 1949, when he obtained a position as a librarian in Charpentras.

1950 sees the publication of his novel *L'Abbé C.*, the first strictly fictional work he has published under his own name, and in 1951 he is appointed keeper at the municipal library in Orleans. In 1953 he works on two works in Skira's 'History of Art' series, one on Manet, the other on the cave paintings at Lascaux in the South of France, both of which are published in 1955, in which year he become seriously ill. The same year he is able to write the novel, *Ma mère*, although it will not be published until after his death.

In 1957 he published *Le Bleu du ciel*, a novel dating back to 1935, as well as *La Litérature et le mal*, a collection of essays, and the book that is perhaps the summation of his life's work, *L'Érotisme*. He spends a lot of energy trying to animate a new review, *Genèse*, which will be devoted to eroticism, but the project is abandoned after a row with his sponsor.

During 1958 he immersed himself in study of the documents relating to the trial of Gilles de Rais. The documents will be published in a translation by Pierre Klossowski, for which Bataille writes an introduction. In 1961 an auction of paintings by friends like Arp, Ernst, Giacometti, Masson, Matta, Michaux, Miró and Picasso was organised to give him some financial security. This enabled him to buy an apartment in Paris. His final book, *Les Larmes d'Eros*, a study of eroticism through painting, was published in the same year. He applies for a transfer of position back to the Bibliothèque Nationale, an application which is granted, but he dies on 8th July 1962 before he can take the post up.

Chapter 3

Themes and intellectual background

Bataille has been seen as a philosopher of excess and transgression concerned with an interrogation of the nature of being and his work has been used to legitimate extremes of behaviour. To see his work solely in this light, however, is to fall prey to a misunderstanding. Certainly Bataille saw excess as a path of awareness, and one that was far more fruitful than that of asceticism, but nevertheless he did not consider excess in isolation from a sense of order. He was not at all an advocate of unlimited excess. Indeed he was a rather discreet and reticent man who had a strong puritanical element in his make-up.[1]

Bataille believed that existence was essentially paradoxical and it is this that gives his work its 'impossible' character, something that is sometimes unintentionally emphasised by the fact that Bataille can be an inconsistent thinker. He scorned the calculation that would have given his work an overall shape or created the illusion of internal logical consistency (which would have implied a project to which one would devote oneself and to which one would thereby become subservient and unable to serve the total needs of knowledge). As a basically self-taught philosopher, Bataille drew on a wealth of influences that can appear at first sight to co-exist uneasily in his thought.

As he saw the nature of existence itself as being paradoxical, so in many ways Bataille himself was a paradoxical figure who liked to confound expectations. We will often find that wherever we want to place him, he will not be there. He embraced contradiction as a condition of life and there is something of the Dr Jekyll and Mr Hyde about his character, with the difference that he was fully aware of the different aspects of his personality. He entered into excess and debauchery at the same time as he was working as a sober librarian at the Bibliothèque Nationale, whilst assiduously studying philosophy. Although André Breton accused him of being an 'obsessive' (an accusation that had, as Bataille accepted, some truth at the time, when he was obsessed with images of violent excremental convulsions), there was never anything of the sexual obsessive about him: he entered into debauchery with all the seriousness and diligence of a novice priest taking a vow of chastity. In many ways, Bataille was never anything other than the serious young man who would have devoted himself to God. But the focus changed with his loss of faith: he devoted himself to atheism (or, as he called it, an 'atheology') instead. There was nothing compulsive about his plunge into debauchery. Rather he had a need to confront the dark forces of the unconscious, and test the limits of being. He approached this task almost in the way of a scientific experiment: it responded to the need to experience the extreme. Nevertheless, he was not seduced by this extreme.

His writing displays the same quality of paradox. We are never sure of our ground and often it seems that it is about to slip away. He plunged into writing with a remarkable sense of diligence and gravity. There can be no doubt that Bataille is an authentic thinker who cared very deeply about his work. As a philosopher he was largely self-taught, as he was in all the other spheres of his intellectual activity. He speaks to us in a tone of intimacy and familiarity and demands our recognition

Do we classify him basically as a novelist (that is a literary man), as a philosopher, as a poet, a historian of art, an economist, a theologian, a political theorist or as an anthropologist? In many ways he was all of these, and yet none of them. Do we need to classify him at all? I think it is important to do so, not to confine his work to a narrow context, but to emphasise the central concerns of his work, around which all the multi-farious strands of his thought radiate. To this extent he is essentially a social philosopher. All of his writings, even those that seem furthest removed from social concerns, like his poetry or the often gnomic reflections of *Inner Experience*, are concerned with the nature of man's collective being and how his individual aspirations respond to it. Even in his most obviously personal writings the aim is to see beyond individual consciousness into social conditions and the life of the collectivity. He has no interest in being itself, or in the individual isolated in his freedom. The former is irrelevant, since being can never be dissociated from social circumstances. To this extent he is much closer to Marx than to, say, Heidegger. The question Heidegger asked: 'Why is there being and not nothingness?', was meaningless to Bataille. Or rather it was a question he had answered in a preliminary and yet decisive way: there is being *because* there is nothingness. He did not believe that the individual, isolated from social processes, actually exists.

Psychologically, Bataille's sensibility was in accord with the social unity of societies which, when they banish someone from their community, consider that the person has ceased to exist. In itself existence has no meaning. Humanist ideology meant little to him. A human being who thinks he exists in an independent way, that is, separately from others, is living under a delusion: individuality is conferred only through the social and any being that is separate from collective standards cannot be human. Existence is a material given that is at one with the essence of a person's being. The two can never be separated and it is vain to seek any meaning for being other than in social relations. Bataille's position is at the same time a refusal of all hope placed in any form of transcendence. What was essential for him was to face one's social and existential reality as squarely as one could and not strive to elude the inevitability of one's fate. The problem of existence does not lie in being but in socialisation. Bataille's work is embodied in a profound rejection of the 'why' of existence, which he perceived as a sickness of rationality. It is vain and naive to think we can understand anything that exists beyond our own existential framework and so he can assert in *Eroticism*, that it 'is not necessary to solve the riddle of existence. It is not even necessary to ask it.'[2]

This emphasises the sociological and anthropological aspects of his thought, and he always gravitated towards sociological study, but where he differs from most anthropologists or sociologists is that his data always begins, not with an external other, established as an object of study, but with himself and his own inner sensibility. He does not analyse given data with a view to drawing a theory from it. Rather his 'theory' (if it can be so designated, in so far as he eschewed the calculations of grand theoretical plans) is drawn from within himself, projected outwards. The basis for this point of view is contained in a fundamental immanence of being and a monist vision of the world: he has no conceptual framework for dealing with plurality or the notion of an otherness that is not contained within one's own being. Life is one and any separation of elements from the totality of being by definition implied error.

In tracing his intellectual genealogy, we should perhaps begin with Durkheim, who provides the starting-point for Bataille's own sociology. As we know, Durkheim deified the social, making it the only measurement for the classification of sociological phenomena. For Durkheim individuals in themselves were unable to provide sociological data because society itself, being a compound of individuals, was qualitatively quite different from the sum of the individuals that comprised it.

The basis for social analysis, therefore, had to be the collectivity and the first task for the sociologist was to determine the nature of the social fact constituted by the particular collectivity. Psychology was thus irrelevant to sociological analysis. For Bataille, Durkheim's characterisation of societies as different in quality from the sum of their parts was an important point, and he therefore refused to accept that it was possible to study the whole through its parts. Since we are part of the human society that, as sociologists, we study, it is not possible for us to stand entirely outside the whole and view it from that perspective. We need also to take into account our own relation with that whole. But more importantly, it is also necessary to examine one's own inner sensibility and to project the society through one's own experience, whilst recognising the extent to which the conditions of that external society are necessarily qualitatively different from the sum of one's own experience.

To appreciate fully what this means, we need to take a closer look at the background against which Bataille worked. This brings us back to surrealism. The fundamental principle of surrealism was set out clearly by André Breton in the *Second Manifesto*: 'Everything tends to make us believe that there exists a point of the mind at which life and death, real and imaginary, past and future, communicable and incommunicable, high and low, cease to be perceived contradictorily.' This statement relies upon the essential oneness of the universe and of our own experience within it. It draws in particular upon two sources: the Hegelian dialectic, based as it is on the complementarity of opposites, and the science of alchemy, which took for its principle the hermetic principle that 'whatever is below is like what is above and that whatever is above is like what is below'. This principle is based on the supposition that all things are interconnected and that it is possible to discover the correspondences between them. There can be no question that Bataille accepted this principle as the basis of his thought. Without it his thinking as a whole makes little sense.

From this perspective, Bataille treated 'society' as what he called a 'compound being'. He explored this in a presentation to the College of Sociology:

A human society, is in the world as a distinct, but not isolated, existence. It is distinct not only from the rest of things and beings but also from other societies: It is composed of a multitude of elements that are more or less identical to those that compose the neighbouring society, but they belong to it in a sufficiently stable manner.[3]

This idea was something common to surrealism and was explored with the greatest precision by Pierre Mabille in his book *Égrégores ou la vie des civilisations*.[4] An '*égrégore*' is a expression taken from alchemy and refers to the third term that is established from the conjoining of two different elements. It works on the chemical principle of precipitation. Water, for instance, is an *égrégore* of hydrogen and oxygen. Likewise, a child is an *égrégore* created by the encounter of a man and a woman, a society an *égrégore* born from the encounter of disparate individuals, a civilisation an *égrégore* born from the encounter of different societies. In each case the principle is the same: the resulting *égrégore* is simultaneously the same as and yet qualitatively different from the elements of which it is comprised. In applying this schema, then, we need to take care not to confuse the different status of *égrégores*. Even if they work on the same principle, the component parts of a society do not interrelate in the same way as the parts of a human body, but have their own dynamic which has to be drawn out. Differentiation is therefore of crucial importance, but it needs to be recognised that differentiation is a methodological classification and nothing more: it does not change the principle underlying the unity of the world. For Mabille the process of being born was a projection of oneself onto the universe. It was not a matter of our being thrown into the world with no will of our own: in effect the universe itself is reborn at the moment of each person's birth.

For Mabille, then, there is no conflict between internal being and external reality. The individual is the internalisation of the universe as the universe is the externalisation of the individual. Any change can therefore only be explained by the force of desire which acts (both within the individual and within the collectivity) on the chemical principle of precipitation.

Mabille's conception is more worked out, but its principle is identical with what Bataille believed. It assumes that the fundamental elements of the world are the same and that there is in essence no difference between social and personal being.

With this emphasis on society we might assume that Bataille's thought remains strictly within the tradition of Durkheim. Nevertheless, such an assertion would be problematic. If it is true that Durkheimian sociology was his starting point and that Durkheim provided a confirmation of his view that the social was more than the sum of its parts, there is much in Durkheim that dissatisfied Bataille. As we know, Durkheim went further than the assertion that the social was more than the sum of its parts, to found the social as the only reality that could be subject to sociological analysis, since it was only through social interaction that social facts could be created. Since such social facts could not be reduced to their constituent parts, psychology could play no part in sociological analysis.

Bataille agreed that the social was the only reality of the individual, but he did not accept Durkheim's reductionism, which left the problem half way, since he considered the movement to be dual; so that if the social served to define the reality of the individual, then it follows that it must equally be the case that the individual was the only reality of the social. In addition, the individual was not merely a part of the social, but was itself a social whole having the same methodological status as society. We have said that being was essentially social for Bataille, but equally it followed that the movement was dual: social reality had meaning only in the actions of the individuals that comprised it.

For Bataille, therefore, no analytical distinction was made between individuals and collectivities. The collective was not an abstraction but a reality that was no less distinctive in its essential characteristics than a particular individual. Furthermore, the dynamic nature of the relation between individual and collective worked, as we have seen, on universal principles so that the relation of individual to collective was of the same order as that of cells in a body to the individual. Against the common tendency to perceive individual consciousness as being clearly defined, but collective consciousness, if it existed at all, as an abstraction, Bataille perceived no essential difference between the two: a society was as clearly, or as indistinctly, defined as an entity as was an individual. If collective consciousness is difficult to define, it is no more so than that of the individual. He expressed this as follows: 'the knowledge of what we call consciousness results only in a very vague notion, which is such that we have no right at all to dispute that society itself has a consciousness.'[5] In his work, Bataille therefore individualises collectivities, which have their own motives and desires, which, although they extend from those of the individuals that comprise them, remain qualitatively different from them. A collectivity nevertheless 'thinks' in exactly the same way as does an individual, even if the context of its thought responds to its own contingencies, which are necessarily different from those of any of the individuals comprised within it. Its reality is therefore necessarily more than that of the actors within it.

In this respect, Bataille's conception is closer to Marx than to Durkheim. Like Marx he did not separate man from society, nor did he separate society from nature. Marx's comments on the relation of individual to collectivity are very illuminating in relation to Bataille's (and Mabille's) thinking:

It is above all necessary to avoid once more establishing "society" as an abstraction over against the individual. The individual *is* the *social being*. His vital expression – even when it does not appear in the direct form of a *communal* expression, conceived in association with other men – is therefore an expression and confirmation of *social life*. Man's individual and species-life are not two *distinct things*, however much – and this is necessarily so – the mode of existence of individual life is a more *particular* or a more *general* mode of species-life, or species-life a more *particular* or more *general* individual life.[6]

This defines exactly the way that Bataille methodologically approaches his material: a society or an ideological concept is an entity itself, which, depending on the circumstances under investigation, is examined in its particular or general characteristics in a way that responds directly to but without being determined by the life of its individual components. Unlike Durkheim, Bataille therefore does not fetishise society against the individual, but treats both society and individual as being of equal methodological importance.

The objection may be that if we consider a concept like, for instance, Christianity, as a living process rather than abstraction, does this not mean that we are prey to a delusion since even a cursory glance at Christian beliefs soon reveals a vast number of conflicts and incompatibilities that immediately seem to show that to treat Christianity as a 'whole' must be absurd? Unlike a human being a concept such as Christianity has no integral reality that can be conceptualised as an independent entity.

This problematic has force, however, only in so far as we consider the human being itself to be an independent, homogeneous entity. For Bataille it was not at all apparent that this was so. Do not the elements within the human body respond to each other through often conflicting and antagonistic behaviour? Is it any more possible to define the human individual in its pristine state than it is a concept like Christianity? It is impossible to determine the point at which the human body begins or ends. Yet despite the mass of surging conflicts within it somehow there is a centre that holds together in a way that makes it possible for us to perceive each human individual as a separate entity differentiated from all others.

To determine the specificity of that individual it is necessary to separate out the essential elements that go to make up the individual. The same thing is true for any collectivity. This is not to assert that it is possible to establish a collectivity's true reality, since any such discussion is framed through another's subjectivity and is inevitably distorted by the position of the subject making the observation of it. It is especially difficult for us to make an observation of a social whole of which we ourselves are a part and it is therefore necessary to take account of the distortion that is brought by one's own perspective on the material. The different nature of collectivities lies in the fact that where individual entities have the same form as us and respond in large part to the same exigencies as we do, collectivities are shaped from different exigencies which are less easily perceptible to us. This means that it is all the more difficult for us to determine the boundaries of collectivities.

To this extent Bataille would doubtless agree with Weber that such collectivities are ideal types and their realities are purely conceptual and subject to sudden collapse. Nevertheless, they retain their reality as clear entities. They are not at all fictions.

Although it may seem that Bataille's starting point is incompatible with Weber, there is a point at which his methodology becomes at one with the conceptualisation of ideal types that Weber put forward as the basis for a *particular* viewpoint that has no methodological reality in itself separate from the observation made of it. It seems highly likely that Bataille was influenced by Weber in this respect, since he certainly knew Weber's work from discussions with his friend Jules Monnerot, who had fully assimilated Weber's theory of social science, something he put to good effect in his trenchantly anti-Durkheimian critique *Les Faits sociaux ne sont pas des choses* (1946), in which Monnerot argued that social facts must always be considered to be living beings and not the 'things' to which Durkheim had reduced them.

Before considering how this understanding of the relation of collective to individual affects Bataille's practice, let us glance at the other influences on Bataille in his formative years.

As already mentioned, Bataille had little formal philosophical training. Prior to 1922, when he discovered Nietzsche, he seems to have been largely uninterested in philosophical thought and to have made little formal study of it. We should perhaps recall that at this time French thought was remarkably parochial and drew on a stagnant nineteenth-century tradition that remained ignorant of if not hostile to the German tradition issuing from Hegel. Certainly Bataille's initial exposure to philosophy in 1922 through Bergson (who he met in London) was not to his taste and did not encourage an interest in philosophy. It was not until he met the Russian emigré philosopher Leon Chestov in 1923 and became his pupil that he found a path into philosophical thinking. Although little remembered today, and hardly known in English,[7] Leon Chestov was a marginal but important intermediary figure as the tide of French philosophy turned from its inward nineteenth-century tradition that had culminated in Bergsonian idealism towards German philosophy. Chestov had a dark view of the world perfectly suited to Bataille's temperament. He had fled from the USSR after the Bolshevik Revolution and his resolute anti-idealism set him apart from the spirit of the times and undoubtedly marked Bataille's thinking in a profound way, to the extent that he never appears to have properly appreciated what idealism really was and failed to realise that his own philosophy contained a very strong idealist tinge. Apart from having a crucial influence on Bataille, Chestov was the key influence on another marginal on the fringes of surrealism, the Romanian philosopher Benjamin Fondane, and in many ways, Chestov played a role in a Bataille's life that was analogous to that of René Guénon in André Breton's. There is much that connects Chestov and Guénon, even if they appear at first to be very different. Both were resolutely anti-modern, reactionary in the best sense, castigating the 'idols' of science, technology, progress and rationalism. But where Guénon looked to the East to formulate a critique of Western decadence, Chestov's models were Pascal, Dostoyevsky, Nietzsche and the Bible.

Chestov really gave Bataille his first lessons in philosophy and revealed the marvel of Nietzsche's philosophy to him. Although Bataille later minimised the extent of Chestov's influence on him, it is apparent that it remained considerable and that Bataille's understanding of Nietzsche was very much the result of Chestov's teachings, to the extent that it could be said that Bataille continued to see Nietzsche through Chestov as much as he was later to see Hegel through Alexandre Kojève.

Chestov's philosophy was based on a rejection of knowledge and its replacement with faith. For Chestov the great enemy was causation, which he considered to be a lie that had deluded people into believing they could master the universe by means of understanding. Science and speculative philosophy had destroyed man's fundamental freedom, which was endowed upon them by God. The root of evil is the obsession with acquiring knowledge, which turns men away from God, for whom 'all things are possible'. The modern age was thus a nightmare of godlessness. Its remedy was a return to faith, but faith that asserted revolt, since the essence of faith was a refusal to accept necessity. Distinctions between good and evil or truth and falsehood were thereby irrelevant. But, following Nietzsche, this recovery of God could only be accomplished by first passing through his own nothingness. If one accepted that God did not exist, it becomes essential to take God's place, to become God oneself, since one was faced with a nothingness in which all things needed to be created. Faith becomes equated with an audacity to defy necessity so that distinctions of good and evil, truth and false-hood become irrelevant.

These elements are clearly crucial for Bataille and it is obvious that Chestov's conception of philosophy at the extremes of human behaviour must also have been a revelation to a Bataille who was only just freeing himself from the rigours of ascetic Christianity. In Chestov's thought, we can already see the germ of Bataille's idea of 'inner experience'. In the immediate though, Chestov imbued Bataille with his own violent anti-idealism and caused him to recognise the necessity of following Dostoyevsky's prescription 'all is permitted'. Was it from Chestov that he took upon himself the need to supplement his everyday existence as a librarian with a double life in which he determined to experience life at the edge of being, which went as far as experimenting with Russian roulette?[8]

One of the great enemies of the human spirit according to Chestov was Hegel, and this also coloured Bataille's early feelings towards the master of Jena. Instinctively Bataille rebelled against the idealist elements in Hegel's thought and also against the totalising elements that led to the possibility of completion within the terms of his system. Bataille found the idea of the 'end of history' somewhat absurd; this in fact was a source of conflict between him and Kojève. At the same time there were elements in Hegel that were too powerful for Bataille to resist, and we must not underestimate the importance of Hegel to Bataille, even if he remained doubtful about aspects of Hegel's philosophy. It should be said also that his Hegel was one refracted through the teachings of Alexandre Kojève, whose teaching had an overwhelming effect on him. Although he wanted to understand the totality of experience, Bataille hated the idea of reducing totality to a calculated project and this aspect of Hegel's thought did not interest him or perhaps even repelled him. But he was seduced by Hegel's dialectical method, especially the dialectic of master and slave, which was the focus of Kojève's teachings and became an essential element in Bataille's thought. As he said, Hegel's master and slave relation is

the decisive moment in the history of consciousness of self and, it must be said, to the extent that we have to distinguish between each thing that affects us, no one knows anything of *himself* if he has not understood this movement which determines and limits man's successive possibilities.[9]

If we wish to understand Bataille's thought, it is essential that we appreciate the particularity of his relation to Hegel since it may be said that his thinking takes shape through Hegel. This relation was not an entirely harmonious one, since Bataille was both magnetised and repelled by Hegel's concepts.

Complementary to Hegel, and towards whom Bataille in many ways displayed a similar ambivalence, was the disquieting figure of the Marquis de Sade. From Sade, Bataille took an absolute sense of revolt, a sensibility that asserted how essential it was not to allow oneself to be subordinated to the world. Sade's attitude towards writing was also crucial, asserting that one must write from necessity and through one's own body. And of course, the quality of marginality, willingly accepted by Sade no matter what the personal cost, and his utter refusal to conform or submit to uncongenial conditions, was something that marked Bataille very strongly.

The other main influences were Marx and the surrealists, both crucial in bringing into the frame, in very different ways, the importance of the social. Marx's notion of social being is that of the communist *community* that will supersede the capitalist reality based on the demands of personal interest that Bataille rejected in an unconditional way.

From surrealism, even from the beginnings when he was hostile to surrealism as an idea, Bataille likewise recognised the germ of a new sense of collective values and realised how essential the nature of the surrealist community was. The community of which surrealism was the embryo was one that sought to give form to a heterogeneous conception of community that went against the essentially homogeneous nature of the dominant capitalist reality and as such served as a complement to Bataille's idea of what communism represented.

All these influences took shape through Nietzsche, whose work provides one of the keys to Bataille's thought, and whose example was the greatest intellectual influence on Bataille. For Bataille, Nietzsche was less a philosopher than a friend, or perhaps a sort of spiritual guide, someone to whom he could turn when things became difficult: all of his work is essentially a conversation with the German thinker. It is perhaps not accurate to speak of influence here, for it was really a question of love. Bataille made it clear that the affinity he felt with Nietzsche lay 'in a very particular kind of experience apparently proper to both Nietzsche and myself . . . I believe there to be a relation between the thought of Nietzsche and my own, analogous to that which exists in a community.'[10] Yet we should take care not to allow the intimacy that Bataille felt with Nietzsche to blind us to the fact that Bataille nevertheless displaces Nietzsche in so far as he renounces or ignores both the will to power and the notion of the eternal return, concepts which many commentators have considered to be essential to Nietzsche's philosophy. In addition, Bataille is rather out on a limb with regard to Nietzsche scholarship, in so far as he considers that what mattered for Nietzsche was not the individual but society. In many ways, therefore, Bataille's relation with Nietzsche might be seen to be as problematic as his relation with Hegel.

As a thinker, Bataille uses key terms which we need to be aware of in relation to the way his thought develops. If the essential element in Bataille's thinking is the social, it may be said that the recreation of communal being is his most immediate concern. This should be borne in mind as we consider his work as a whole.

To end this overview of Bataille's background, let us take the key words in his thought and offer a preliminary explanation for how he conceives of these concepts.

The fundamental element that makes possible the unity and continuance of society is the *sacred*, and it is the idea of the sacred that is consequently the most important of all Bataille's concepts, the pivot around which all of his thought revolves. Here Bataille is at his most Durkheimian, taking the distinction between sacred and profane as an essential methodological tool. No society could exist without the sacred, which was the cement that held a given society together.

For Durkheim the separation between sacred and profane was absolute to an extent than no other distinction could be. Where concepts like good and evil reflected each other by belonging to the same order (i.e. morality) sacred and profane could never be mingled. Something could only be either sacred or profane: there could be no graduation between them. To pass from one to the other therefore required a transformation: a profane thing had to be purified and have its essence transformed before it could become sacred.

Bataille largely accepted Durkheim here and the sacred for Bataille is the unifying aspect of society, taking shape where people need to offer themselves up in a sacrificial consecration to the values of the collectivity. The sacred is the forbidden element of society that exists at the margin where different realities meet. Without it society could not exist, for if it was lacking then Bataille asserts that 'the totality of the plenitude of being escapes man, [and] he would henceforth be only an incomplete man'. The sacred is not for Bataille a characteristic of revealed religion, but an essential element of social solidarity. It is thereby equated with the need for communication.

The sacred takes concrete form through people's need for a meaningful *communication*. This was for Bataille the means by which the cohesion of society was maintained. Without communication there could be no society. It was through communication, therefore, that the immediate needs of the isolated being are linked with those of all others within a given society. Through communication the selfish pursuit of individual gain is perceived to be unacceptable to social well-being and it becomes possible to conceive of genuine social bonding.

Different aspects of a society's structure are designated by Bataille under sociological terms that have traditionally been used to describe the way social cohesion functions. Bataille uses the words *homogeneity* and *heterogeneity* in what at first appears a fairly orthodox way, but as we look into these concepts they can be seen to gain elements that are unique to him. His starting point is Tönnies' distinction between *gesellschaft* (which is equated with homogeneity) and *gemeinschaft* (equated with heterogeneity). This distinction can be expressed as between an organised society based upon inflexible law and cohesion (*gesellschaft*) and one based upon social forms of co-operation, custom and ritual expression (*gemeinschaft*).

Bataille also used this distinction in a qualitative way to provide a critique of capitalist society: while all societies display an impulse towards social homogeneity in some form, this is generally resisted through a heterogeneous structuring. In capitalism, though, homogeneity is welcomed and indeed imposed by means of an economic accumulation that has a totalitarian function, so that present-day society becomes uniquely homogeneous in a way that causes all aspects of its fabric and its very nature to reduce people to their social roles, so denying them the communal effusion to be discovered in the heterogeneous activity that is essential to true communication, thereby tending to destroy any creativity and collective effervescence that does not serve a useful purpose. Present-day society was thus based upon calculation and industry, which considered the principle of exchange and individual integrity to be determining factors. Against this, a heterogenous society, or more specifically one that took the heterogeneous into account and did not try to reduce itself to homogeneity, was based upon flexible structures based in participation and co-operation which did not forcibly reduce people to their social functions, but allowed their social functions to grow organically from their own natural inclinations. Homogeneity is thus the path to social disintegration.

A heterogeneous society needed to take account not only of what occurred within its heart, but also of what was distant from it and existed on its margins. It needed, that is, to engage with the sacred. In reducing itself to its functions, a homogeneous society leads to the destruction of the idea of religion and so denies the sacred in a direct way. By so doing, it denies itself, since the sacred lies at the heart of social being.

As the sacred exists at the margin, at the point where different realities meet, so a heterogeneous society needs to take account of those points of intersection, which have been expelled from the structure of the integral body. Thus the sacred is revealed in bodily exhalations (blood, sweat, tears, shit); extreme emotions (laughter, anger, drunkenness, ecstasy); socially useless activity (poetry, games, crime, eroticism), all of which take the form of a heterology that homogenous society would like to definitively expel. Against this homogenising process, Bataille put forward the possibility of a 'science of heterology', defined as being whatever is irremediably 'other'.

The sacred is also the forbidden aspect of society, crystallising the moment of rupture between one thing and another. The anguish of being leads mankind to establish interdictions to control the effusiveness and prodigality of life. But in a heterogeneous society these interdictions do not imply the denial of what they prohibit. Instead they assert the value of the forbidden, which is allowed free play at times of *transgression*, a festival of expenditure and loss that complements the need for work and the rule of law.

For Bataille the notion of a heterogeneous society, in which social hierarchy is denied, was represented by the acephale, an old gnostic divinity that symbolised matter as an active principle.

These elements of social being are complemented by factors that relate more to the particularities of personal being.

Death needs to be understood in Bataille's specific sense. For him death was an active principle. It did not simply mean the cessation of life. Rather death was the completion of life; its aim and dissolution. It was also the negation of life; its condition and essential quality. Life was nourished from death, which held it in a state of tension. Even as life itself negates death in the moment of reproduction and thereafter seeks to exclude it, death remains as an ever-present active principle that alone makes life possible.

Death brings into play the ideas of *continuity* and *discontinuity*. By these concepts Bataille seeks to show the essential quality of being in the world. To live is to exist within limits. Being, therefore, always accords with the limit that defines it. To the extent that it is conscious of itself as existing, being contemplates the idea of not existing with horror. In consequence it strives always to maintain the sense of its own existence as an independent essence.

However, this existence is incomplete since it separates itself from whatever is other from it. If it is an entirely independent being, it can understand nothing outside of itself. To understand its situation in the world it needs to engage with an other from whom it perceives its separation while at the same time desiring unity with it (this is the importance of communication). Our essence is thus to be incomplete beings. The result is that the limited, discontinuous being, even as it strives to assert its own being and independence, aspires to achieve a state of continuity with what is external to it. This unity is impossible: by achieving its desire of continuity such a being would destroy the very independence which it experiences as its unique and essential personality. But at the same time individual isolation is an imposture. In this sense we always strive towards what will destroy us; our condition is one of loss. We are always living on the edge of an abyss.

Discontinuity is the condition of life, but this discontinuity emerges from out of a lost continuity to which we will one day return. But as incomplete beings we strive vainly to overcome the limits that define us. We are defined by the extent of our sense of *anguish*, which is marked by an urge towards what is *impossible*.

Anguish, for Bataille is thus a fundamental condition of existence. It is an inescapable element of our being, announced by the birth pangs that accompany the rending moment of our coming into the world. At the same time it is the recognition of the incompleteness of being, the yearning for a lost continuity and a striving to go beyond being. As Bataille defined it, anguish is 'the sentiment of a danger connected to the inextinguishable expectation'.[11] This sense of anguish is thus at once a sense of loss and profusion. It is present within us not as a negative weight that bears down on us, but as an urge to go beyond our limits, for it is the sense of limits that defines our existence whilst at the same time being connected with the nakedness of existence, a nakedness that for Bataille was rending and painful.

According to Sarane Alexandrian, Bataille established an 'ontology of nudity',[12] and this is another of Bataille's important concepts. *Nudity*, for Bataille, did not signify a natural state, but its opposite, emphasising our discomfiture over discontinuity. The sense of shame we feel in our nakedness is the beginning of communication and crystallises the urge of love. Naturism was considered absurd by Bataille since dress was an essential element of our being (which we will recall is exclusively social in nature). When we take off our clothes we pare away a part of our personality. Undressing is thus a solemn act, and it is this that explains its connection in Bataille's mind with the act of thinking and writing. The idea of there being a natural state from which we are separated by social conventions and which can be recovered by laying ourselves bare is a particularly pernicious form of puritanism for Bataille, for whom nudity is rather a laceration, a terrifying shattering of our being. When we are naked we are faced with the anguish of our origins and our incompleteness: naked, we contemplate an inadequacy at the heart of ourselves. Anyone who does not feel a sense of shame when naked is, in Bataille's view, denying their sense of humanity and surrendering to a displaced form of repression. Bataille expresses the intoxication of nudity in these terms:

> The fact of both parties being lowered together with the pleasures of nakedness alters this state, and the nakedness of each of the lovers is then reflected in the mirror each is to the other. Its a slow delight-filled vertigo prolonging the vertigo of the flesh.[13]

But the corollary of nudity is the *impossible*, a state that offers a sense of overflowing, of repletion. It encapsulates the paradox of existence, since our essential motivation (motivated, that is, by anguish) is to go beyond our limits and yet, at the same time, it is apparent that if we were to do so we should in fact cease to exist. The most we can do, therefore, is to experience the vertigo at the edge on which our life unfolds.

This bring us to the most problematic of Bataille's concepts and one which endeavours to bring together both the personal and social aspects of Bataille's thought. This is the idea of *sovereignty*. The basic definition is simple enough: it is the opposite of servility. However, difficulties arise when one tries to conceptualise this in practice (the same difficulties would doubtless arise if one was to try to define *servility* in the same way). Bataille struggled with this in the third part of *The Accursed Share* (entitled 'Sovereignty'), which is perhaps his most unsatisfactory book. We will deal with the problems it raises later. For now we will simply sketch what Bataille meant by this concept.

Bataille's starting point for the notion of sovereignty is the Hegelian dialectic of slave and master, but Bataille goes beyond Hegel in one crucial respect. For Hegel the master obtains his mastery by preferring death to subservience, while the slave prefers subservience to death, but for Hegel the master cannot obtain liberty because he is bound by the slave's recognition and is never able to gain the experience of slavery. The master must therefore remain an incomplete being. The slave, on the other hand, has the possibility of revolt, and it is only through such revolt he may gain the experience that makes of him a complete, that is, a truly sovereign person.

For Bataille this this is insufficient, since he perceives that work is essentially servile and therefore the experience of work is not a proper basis for sovereignty. The slave can only gain sovereignty by a rejection of work. To become sovereign it is necessary, in Bataille's view, both to refuse power and to reject anything that would, like work, be used as a means to such an end. Only the means in itself can be sovereign. Indeed, sovereignty may be said to be the determination to have done with ends and live entirely in the instant. It represents an existence freed from worry, in which utilitarian principles are considered to be of no account. It also implies being able to recognise one's own insignificance and laugh at the fact.

In this connection, we also need to be aware of Bataille's idea of *non-knowledge* or *un-knowing*, which may be said to bear the same relation to knowledge as anti-matter bears towards matter. The rational accumulation of knowledge was, by definition, false: as knowledge accumulates, so it simultaneously moves away from itself. This is a rejection of genius and the idea of the wise man. For Bataille there could be no knowledge that did not bring with its is own form of ignorance. Here again we see the importance of Chestov's influence, since it was one of the central planks of Chestov's philosophy that the evil of knowledge has corrupted the heart of Western man and there was a need to undermine it with faith. In this (as in most other respects) Bataille reacted against the conclusive nature of Chestov's condemnation, but he retained the actual framework established by Chestov and worked through it.

For Bataille, we should perhaps repeat, the condition of life is paradox in its essence. Our existence itself is impossible. We should, in fact, not be able to exist at all, and yet, somehow, we do so in an equilibrium that, while it remains precarious, nevertheless has something of a miraculous quality. This paradox is the true 'impossibility' of the universe. Because of this paradoxical nature, the 'why' of existence is irrelevant. For Bataille the only possible response to being was laughter.

Chapter 4

Towards a sociology of abundance

We have noted how Bataille's attitude towards science was ambivalent. He was doubtful about scientific methodology and suspicious of its intentions, yet at the same time he sought to frame his own work in relation with established science and continued to maintain that scientific objectivity was the only path of knowledge. On the other hand, he did not see any value in the pursuit of knowledge for itself. Too often, he felt, those drawn to science lacked passion: 'Science is made by men in whom the desire to understand is dead.'[1] Equally he denied the claims that science made for disinterested knowledge. Science could too easily succumb to servility and betray its own findings. It needed first of all to be true to itself and learn not to serve. In addition, he believed that a genuine knowledge needed to recognise its own essential incompleteness and the fact that it had to be completed through the embrace of a complementary 'non-knowledge', so that the known loses itself in a plunge into the unknown. Everything in Bataille is directed against any idea of absolute knowledge. The need to explore the interplay between knowledge and non-knowledge, arising in Bataille's mind from the fact that he recognised the needs of science and yet refused to allow them to become overwhelming, is crucial to an understanding of the way Bataille conceived of his intellectual undertaking.

Because the extent of his distrust of scientific methodology is considerable, this has led to his being viewed as a subversive figure who wanted to undermine traditionally accepted scholarly method. It is one of the reasons why post-modernism would like to claim him. However, what seems clear is that no matter how ambivalent Bataille may have been about the ultimate value of science, he certainly had no desire to reform or destabilise it. To the extent that his doubts were well founded, he did not perceive any remedy other than to refuse scientific activity altogether, since it was the practice itself and the basic postulates upon which it worked that were at fault, rather than any particular methodological approach. It could not be reformed, and to undermine or subvert it would be meaningless. If one objected to it to that extent then one needed to refuse to engage with it. He insisted on the contrary that whenever he used the scientific method himself, then his work had to be judged according to traditional standards.

Essentially the doubts Bataille had about science were twofold. As we have seen, first of all he suspected that the professional status of an academic researcher was inimical to true scholarship. How was it possible to retain the sense of vitality and necessity that was the hallmark of true scholarship if one needed to earn one's bread by such activity? Bataille worked as a librarian for most of his life, but he seems to have chosen this path because he was by nature hostile to any form of a career and saw such a position as a means to make a living while pursuing his committed research in other areas. He often, indeed, seems to consider that the refusal of the security offered by professionalism was a *sine qua non* of undertaking the sort of internal research he wished to pursue.

His other doubt concerned the methodology necessarily used by the sciences to determine the object of study. This of course involves the separation of knowing subject from unknowing object and abstracts the object of study from the totality of social relations in which it is to be found and which are essential to its reality.

Bataille did not dispute that this necessity had its value and that many of the most important findings of scientific research would not have been possible without the systematic framework established by this separation, but at the same time one needed to remain alert to its unsatisfactory elements. Above all it tended to reduce all phenomena to the level of external data, where a true science should aspire towards an understanding that would do justice to both internal and external data.

The period in which Bataille lived was one that was propitious to maverick intellectuals. Or at least it was an environment in which intellectual activity became a necessity and it was not expected that it should be confined to the context of academia. The inter-war years, at least in France, offered to writers and artists a context in which they felt that their work was of vital importance, that what they were doing was not an indulgence or an entertainment, but had a real consequence for human destiny. In such a context a will towards the totality of experience was the rule. Whereas in general it is necessary for people – even artists – to develop their own speciality and gain mastery of their own particular made of expression, during the twenties and thirties such calculation tended to be scorned. Surrealism provided the most conclusive rationale for this luxuriousness and almost all of the surrealist writers and artists expressed themselves in several media. This was something that had such a strong hold during the inter-war years in France that even more orthodox philosophers who matured during this period, like Sartre and Camus, also felt the need to express themselves in novels and plays as well as in philosophical essays.

Bataille, of course, was no exception and his work covers a vast area; philosophical essays, sociological studies, studies of art and literature, economic analysis, novels, poems. In the forties, he even wrote a film script, which he had hoped would be made into a commercial film. In this his work is very much in accord with the general surrealist environment.

As it emerged from out of the Dadaist negation, surrealism sought a re-orientation of human values. Founded as the negation of the Dadaist negation, there could be no question for the surrealists of returning to old literary forms or even of reinventing them. Literature, for them, was finished. This was a decision upon which there was no turning back, but it was a rejection of the ends, not of the means, of literature. Surrealism essentially sought a sort of generalised poetics in which – to over-simplify – art would be treated with the rigour of science and science would be treated to the disrespect of art. As they stated in one of their early declarations: 'We have nothing to do with literature but we are quite capable, when necessary, of making use of it like anyone else.' But how could they make use of literature if they had nothing to do with it? It was Tristan Tzara who made the crucial distinction between art as a 'means of expression', which was rejected, and art as an 'activity of the spirit', which was the domain in which surrealism sought to situate itself.

The foundation of surrealism lay in automatic writing, which was presented from the first as being in the nature of a scientific experiment into the 'true nature of thought'. The need to penetrate into mental phenomena was a feature of early surrealism. The group itself came together through experiments in collective sleeping fits that took place in 1922, sessions that were based upon Charcot's experiments in hypnotism at Salpetrière. These experiments soon got out of hand and were abandoned, but they set a pattern of collective experimentation that would be the hallmark of surrealism over a wide spectrum of activity.

With the constitution of the Surrealist Group itself in 1924, there

was established a Bureau of Surrealist Research, the aims of which were
to

> gather by every appropriate means communications relative to the
> diverse forms that are susceptible to the unconscious activity of the
> mind. No domain is *a priori* specific for this enterprise and
> surrealism proposes to assemble the greatest possible amount of
> experimental data, for a purpose that has not yet become clear. All
> those people in a position to contribute, in whatever way they like, in
> the creation of genuine surrealist archives, are urgently asked to
> come forward: whether they enlighten us on the origin of an
> invention, or offer us an original means of psychic investigation, or
> they evaluate some striking coincidences, or they set out their most
> instinctive ideas about fashion as well as politics, etc, or they want to
> engage in a free critique of morals, or want to limit themselves to
> confiding their strangest dreams or what their dream suggests.[2]

The results were to have been analysed and published in a monthly
journal, but this never came to pass. Nevertheless, *La Révolution
surréaliste* itself was very much a journal of research. To emphasise this
element, Pierre Naville had been responsible for basing the design on
the sober scientific review, *La Nature*. It first issue contained
unmediated dream accounts and automatic texts, notes on various
subjects and an enquiry, the results of which would later be published in
the journal. The enquiry was: 'We live, we die. What part does the will
play in it? It appears that we kill ourselves as we dream. It is not a moral
question that we ask: IS SUICIDE A SOLUTION?'[3]

These research elements were not an affectation that would be
abandoned in time but responded to an essential element within
surrealism which has remained consistent through its history. The aim
of this activity was not scientific in the sense of seeking a closure of
knowledge; it sought a sort of open-ended form of knowledge and did
not seek to establish definitive answers that could be made susceptible
to 'falsification'. Nevertheless, the frame of the investigation remained
strictly scientific and critical. The surrealists were not using scientific
means to explore artistic questions. Rather, they were developing them
for a purpose that was uniquely their own. Thus the scientific aspect of
surrealism, something that has too often been neglected, played an
important part in it from the beginning. Certainly this element was also
important to Bataille for the same reasons and the ambivalences Bataille
displayed with regard to science very much grow out of the general
ambience of surrealism.

For the most part, it was collective experimentation rather than the critique of society that was the determining feature of early surrealism. Breton's own interests were always more inclined towards psychology rather than sociology, and surrealism in this period played a crucial role in the introduction of Freudian psychoanalysis into France.[4] Nevertheless, sociological themes were never far from the surface and were to become manifest with the appearance of the journal *Documents*, which began to be published in 1929.[5]

In his article 'The Moral Meaning of Sociology',[6] written as a review to Jules Monnerot's book *Les Faits sociaux ne sont pas des choses*, published in 1946, Bataille explains how important sociology was to become for his generation. It had seemed to them that society had lost the secret of its cohesion and the result was that individuals felt lost in their own individuality. He admits that interest in the science of sociology may have arisen through disenchantment with surrealism: at least the rejection of literary activity that surrealism had initially been for them left them unsatisfied with the lack of scientific rigour at the heart of surrealism and caused them to suspect surrealism of remaining within the literary sphere despite itself. They craved, therefore, to engage more seriously in scientific analysis (Bataille ruefully notes that at the time they remained oblivious to the fact that scientific activity had its own sterility that was analogous to that of art).

Even so, the urge towards giving a social meaning to their work was something that was very strong throughout surrealism. This led several of the surrealists to take up what may vaguely be referred to as 'experiments in ethnography' and in this respect it is interesting to compare the approach of Michel Leiris, in the course of his trip as part of the Dakar–Djibouti expedition, with Bataille's later exploration of 'inner experience'.

Leiris travelled into the heart of Africa as a reluctant ethnographer. He was drawn by 'a poetic adventure, a method of concrete knowledge, a test, a symbolic means of stopping time by travelling across space so as to contemplate time'. This led Leiris into an adventure in 'autobiography' which is charted mostly in 'Le régle du jeu'. This involved a loss of self and a process of de-centring, a need to place oneself directly in brute matter and confront one's innermost feelings. Although Leiris and Bataille were very close and had common interests, their work offers an interesting contrast. For where Bataille works outwards from internal data, Leiris works in the opposite direction. Starting with the objective data of his everyday life, collected in a systematic way, Leiris moves inwards to engage in a sort of ethnography of the self. Social investigation is often perceptive in Leiris, but invariably superficial. It was not really what interested him. What concerned him above all was how social reality affects him as an individual, how experience creates the idea he has of his own self.

Bataille's interest, on the other hand, is to engage with his inner psyche in a way to make the separation from his fellow beings less acute: he seeks to understand others through his understanding of himself, to transpose his internal insights into a far-reaching social investigation. Their methods are also very different: Bataille's exploring inner experience in a completely unsystematic way, Leiris charts his sensibility with a meticulous and systematic care. Where Bataille threw dice, Leiris methodically organised all of his notes on a card index.

In the later twenties, the primary necessity behind the shift from a concern with inner, psychological nature towards sociology on the part of many of the surrealist writers was due to the realisation of how important it was to understand the determinants of society. This impulse was already latent within surrealism, implied by the sense that all the surrealists shared of an exigence towards community. The whole structure of the Surrealist Group implied this. Against the traditional elitism of the artist (and this distinguishes it from other intellectual movements, which tended towards not the consecration of a collective experience, but rather embodied a principle by which their individual aims were affirmed collectively; that is that where other artistic groups can be described as being essentially *associations*, and as such holding together through an accordance of mutual interests), surrealism took the impersonal form of a *bund*, or a 'secret society'; the importance of this distinction being that the activity of the group was defined by its own interests, not by the interests of those individuals that comprised it.

This point is a crucial one not simply in order to understand surrealism, but also to appreciate the specificity of Bataille's viewpoint. Even if not always explicit within surrealism, the urge towards community that surrealism displayed implied a critique of individualism and the need to re-invent a genuine idea of community. This was what especially drew Bataille to the surrealists. Likewise, according to Bataille, it soon came to be recognised that they faced a situation in which the vital necessity was not so much to defend the rights of the individual, but rather to defend the rights of society against those of the individual. The society of the time was seen as stifling under the constraints imposed by individualist culture and surrealism can be seen as a protest against such constraints. It was this urge towards community that Bataille found most interesting in surrealism.

Again the contrast with Foucault is instructive here since, with Foucault's proclamation of the 'death of man', the idea of a crisis of individualism has come to be widely recognised. Yet Foucault proceeds from a quite different point of view than Bataille. Bataille is not at all anti-individualist. For him, individualism was a necessary ideological construct within Western culture, and one that marked it irrevocably. The denial of individualism was not an issue for Bataille – what was important was to contest its totalising impulse. Foucault's argument in *The Order of Things* turns on semantic distinctions completely alien to Bataille's way of thinking. The wager offered by Foucault that 'man would be erased, like a face drawn in sand at the edge of the sea'[7] would no doubt be dismissed by Bataille as a meaningless affectation. The point for him was quite different and was centred around the fact that at the beginning of the twentieth century individualism had reached a dead end that needed confronting. It had become overbearing. As an ideology, it had assumed no limits and gained an unhealthy ascendency over the social. It was because this had reached such an unacceptable point that society's rights thereby needed to be defended against the oppression of the individual.

It is striking how relevant this remains in respect of the social attitudes under which we are now living. Fifty years ago Bataille was essentially saying what Margaret Thatcher proclaimed in such a vainglorious way: there is no longer any society. But what for Thatcher was the triumph of a principle for which she stood, for Bataille this possibility was something monstrous and disastrous.

In the context of the period, the whole impetus of those who came to surrealism was sustained by the value of undermining individualist culture and creating new social values. This did not imply the renunciation of individualism, but its transformation into the collective sphere. André Masson expressed this aspect when he defined surrealism as 'the collective experience of individualism'. The focus was on the transformation of the individual into a social being who would use that individuality as one element within his social consciousness: he would recognise that his individual being had no meaning in itself but only took shape in relation to that of others. It was this that necessitated an organisation that would provide a framework and an arena in which common endeavour could be consecrated. One of the central aims of surrealism was to found a new myth, and this endeavour turned upon the issue of the social – against rationalist society based upon calculated aims, it was necessary to explore the possibility of a new society based in organic rather than ideological necessities. It is this fact that equally distinguishes surrealism from the various movements of the avant-garde of the time. Although expressionism and futurism both had social aims, these were consecrated through art. Neither movement conceived itself as engaging directly with social reality (we could hardly imagine any expressionists or futurists as sociologists, for instance, as we can with the surrealists). In so far as they had nothing to do with art and yet were quite able to make use of it, the surrealists always refused to use art as a means towards an end. Indeed, the whole impetus of surrealism was directed towards the general frustration of ends, no matter what they might be. As André Breton said: 'Surrealism is not interested in taking into account anything produced alongside it under the pretext of art or even anti-art; of philosophy or anti-philosophy; in a word, anything that does not have for its ultimate aim the annihilation of being into a jewel, internal and unseeing, with a soul no more of ice than of fire.'[8] The point was not to strive towards something, but to be it, to exist in an immediacy that would be its own realisation, so serving to 'annihilate' being into this jewel.

On this point there can be no doubt of Bataille's fundamental accord with surrealism. He made his position clear when he distinguished surrealism from existentialism. Existentialism strives for a liberty founded against constraints; a liberty, that is, that relies on man's conscious decision made against the necessities of existence. Existentialism is thus an assertion of man's individual consciousness against the movement of the world. But Bataille perceived that, for surrealism, on the contrary, liberty lies within existence and is lost only when we work to dominate it, something which serves to subordinate our existence to the unacceptable demands of everyday living. He writes that in surrealism 'the accent is not placed upon the fact of choosing but on the content of the choice proposed . . . liberty is no longer the liberty to choose, but the choice renders a liberty, a free activity, possible.'[9] Freedom of the will is thereby relinquished, since it is the calculated nature of the will that invariably renders freedom problematic. What is important is the seizure of the instant in which freedom manifests itself.

For all of his distrust of scientific method, Bataille nevertheless had a well-organised and scholarly mind and he was well equipped to approach sociological questions from the perspective of a scientist. However, if he accepted the applicability of the scientific method in many areas of life, he perceived a possibly unresolvable problem as regards the domain of the sacred, the domain he especially wished to explore.

The problem lies precisely in the relation of subject to object. In so far as science must abstract the object of its study from the totality of its social relations, does this not necessarily distort the nature of the object? Does not, therefore, scientific methodology distort the very truth it seeks to establish? This is perhaps not unresolvable in so far as one can take such distortion into account. If we bear in mind that all research bears its imprint of our own subjectivity and that such subjectivity remains part of the perception one has of the object, then we can in great part overcome the problem.

However, Bataille asks whether this is in fact possible when it comes to study of the sacred. Since the sacred is precisely defined as being what is not the profane and since the scientific method is expressly founded in the domain of the profane, something implied by its being based on the principle of falsification, it would therefore appear that it is unable to accept anything as being sacred without compromising its fundamental principles. How can it then, in good faith, even claim to be able to speak about the sacred? In order to treat the sacred, must science not by definition turn it into something that is profane and, by so doing, does it not destroy the very object it wants to study? Furthermore, if we accept that the sacred is by definition the totality of the world, and since only what embodies totality can be considered sacred, how can it be subject to the abstraction from totality that is the necessary pre-requisite for scientific analysis? In the vortex of communication in which the essence of the sacred is founded the distinctions that scientific research needs for its methodology are broken down. Faced with reality of the sacred, Bataille asks, how can disinterested knowledge do other than fail at a basic level, since it is constrained to 'itself serve to alter the meaning of what it reveals'.[10]

This was especially important in the context of the present-day world, since the domain of the sacred remained a crucial element within the structure of social life, and yet for methodological reasons this was something to which the sciences appeared condemned to remain blind. If we accept the sacred as a fundamental part of social solidarity without which no society could exist (this is a basic postulate of Durkheimian sociology), how could sociology make any claims to having established a science of society if it excluded from its analysis any consideration of the sacred in its living form? Bataille expresses the 'crisis' in these terms:

In current society, in which rapid changes are often deceptive in so far as they distance us from a world whose ruins and irreplaceable beauty give us only the sense of decline, indeed it seems to us that we lack an essential factor of life. And the science of sociologists, which reveals this lack, not only does not guide the quest that should follow on from it. Its fundamental principles serve to prevent us from even undertaking it.[11]

This led to the sacred inevitably coming to assume a quality of nostalgia rather than experience. To study it inevitably meant that one had to make an abstraction of it and translate it into the terms of a 'lost paradise', and so seek it only in societies that were far from us in time or space. Science could not accept the sacred as something present within its own society. It had to seek it externally and thereby work on the false assumption that ours was a profane society and that the sacred only survived under more primitive forms of society. This went against the Durkheimian principle that the realm of the profane presupposed the sacred, whose negation and confirmation it was. A 'profane' society was therefore a contradiction in terms, since the profane could not exist separately from a domain of the sacred. A society that was 'profane' would in fact not exist since it would have negated itself, at least if Durkheim was right in contending that the sacred was essential to the structure of a society. A sociology that did not engage with the manifestation of the sacred in contemporary life was therefore fatally flawed, and had in effect ceded its appropriate domain to psychology, by means of which the sacred is relegated to the level of the individual unconscious and so is separated from any collective or social forms.

The necessity for a conception of totality by which to study the sacred could only be attained, Bataille believed, by a methodology that would engage directly with the nature of the material at hand. It was necessary not simply to work with the data collected from far-away 'exotic' people. In so far as such material was considered, it should be within the framework of our own society, not treated as an abstract object only existing externally. If other areas of scientific study could be abstracted from social context and treated in isolation, this was impossible for study of the sacred. In this area at least it became absolutely essential to observe data both internally and externally.

How this was to be addressed was the main methodological focus for Bataille's work.

Throughout his life Bataille was always striving towards the creation of a community within which he could achieve a sense of belonging. When he was attacked by André Breton in the *Second Manifesto of Surrealism* he denied that he had any intention to organise the disaffected surrealists against Breton. This may be true, but we are entitled to wonder, since the desire to found a group around him was a strong motivating factor in Bataille's life. In fact, one can often discern an element of envy when Bataille speaks about the cohesiveness of the group that Breton held together for more than forty years. Certainly, Bataille felt regret that none of his groupings, (particularly Contre-attaque, 'The College of Sociology' and Acéphale) managed to sustain the sort of vital collective effervescence and cohesion of the Surrealist Group.

This impulse towards collectivity also plays an essential part in the development of Bataille's own social theory. Since the sacred is a question of communication, it was only by giving one's work a collective dimension that one could have any possibility of gaining access to it. This served to give a further impetus for an engagement with the nature of collectives.

As we discuss Bataille the writer in this context, we should equally not forget Bataille the editor, for one of the most important contributions he made was through the journals he edited, which did serve to bring together disparate individuals in what he always hoped would be a complicitous relation. Bataille's first attempt to create an environment in which issues could be collectively addressed was the journal *Documents* which was published between 1929 and 1931.[12]

The idea for *Documents* appears to have come from conversations between Bataille and Pierre d'Espezal, a fellow librarian at the Bibliothèque Nationale who was the editor of a journal called *Aréthuse* in which Bataille had published some articles on ancient coins (at the Bibliothèque, Bataille had specialised in numismatics, that is the collection of coins no longer in currency). D'Espezal encouraged the art collector Georges Wildenstein to finance a review that would combine art and ethnography and be published by the Musée du Trocadéro, the Paris ethnography museum, which was soon to be demolished and re-born as the Musée de l'Homme.

The titular editor of *Documents* was the art critic Carl Einstein, with Bataille and Georges-Henri Rivière, the director of the Trocadéro, as his editorial assistants. From the first, though, it was apparently Bataille and Rivière who were largely responsible for the content and visual appearance of the journal and the first issues already had Bataille's stamp on them before he was actually given the formal editorship.[13]

Documents took over the documentary aspect of *La Révolution surréaliste*, but Bataille brought to it a greater rigor (aided of course by the fact that he had a far wider range of material as well as greater financial resources at his disposal than the surrealists, since Bataille could call upon the archives of both the Bibliothèque nationale and the Trocadéro[14]). But where the basis of *La Révolution surréaliste* lay in collective and individual experiments centred around automatism, *Documents* devoted itself to a more sociological analysis of cultural phenomena.

The originality of *Documents* (which is doubtless Bataille's contribution) lies in the way it utilises a generalised anthropology to consider the most disparate of data. Its appearance was especially impressive, for the visual material did not simply illustrate the text; it commented upon it and itself functioned as part of the text. Often the illustrations were incongruous or had no direct relation with the text against which they were placed. This type of incongruous juxtaposition had been pioneered in *La Révolution surréaliste*, but it was only with *Documents* that the possibilities were really exploited to their full effect. The effect was to create a sort of dialectic between word and image which served to emphasise how much representation served to distort the nature of the phenomenon which it represented.

One of the features of the journal was a 'dictionary' that appeared in each issue and emphasised peripheral or incongruous meaning of particular concepts. Bataille's hostility to the closed nature of things was made particularly apparent in his definition of 'Formless', which he defined as follows:

A dictionary begins when it no longer gives the meaning of words, but their tasks. Thus *formless* is not only an adjective having a given meaning, but a term that serves to bring down in the world, generally requiring that each thing have its form. What it designates has no rights in any sense and gets itself squashed everywhere, like a spider or an earthworm. In fact, for academic men to be happy, the universe would have to take shape. All of philosophy has no other goal: it is a matter of giving a frock coat to what is, a mathematical frock coat. On the other hand, affirming that the universe resembles nothing and is only *formless* amounts to saying that the universe is something like a spider or spit.[15]

This definition sets out what Bataille aimed to do with *Documents*, which was to restore the sense of the formless to intellectual enquiry and explore the tasks rather than the meaning of words. But what was especially impressive was that in so doing *Documents* did not embrace eclecticism, something which might be the expected result of an encounter between artists and scientists. *Documents* was a serious sociological journal and included in its pages are contributions from some of the leading sociologists and anthropologists of the day. But it is also a genuine surrealist journal. As editor of *Documents*, Bataille embraced the formless as a positive value, exploring it in a perfectly scientific way. In looking at *Documents* one never feels that there is any conflict between its different elements, which all relate together in a sense of generalised anthropology.[16] What was envisaged, as the flyer issued for its launch announced, was:

> the most disturbing phenomena, those whose consequences have not yet been defined. In this different investigation, the sometimes absurd nature of the results or methods, far from being concealed, as always happens in conformity with the rules of seaminess, will deliberately be stressed, as much through a hatred of platitude as through a sense of the comic.[17]

A unique project, then, that brought together a wide spectrum of writers from the dissident surrealists to ethnologists and art critics, *Documents* was, as Michel Leiris said, made in Bataille's image and as such was 'impossible':

> a Janus publication turning one of its faces toward the higher spheres of culture (of which Bataille was willy-nilly a native through his vocation as well as his training) and the other toward a wild place into which one ventured without any sort of geographical map or passport.[18]

The effect of *Documents* – which was subtitled 'Archaeology, Fine Arts, Ethnography, Miscellanies' – was to offer a sort of ethnography of the everyday in which there was a two-way movement between the exotic and the commonplace. A new materiality emerged, which Bataille defined as 'base-materialism'. This was a concept derived from gnosticism (which he had become interested in through his study of old coins), and Bataille defined it as being whatever is 'external and foreign to ideal human aspirations'.[19] Bataille's strategy was to reduce everything to the same 'low' level.

The study of so-called primitive and exotic peoples was given no privileged status as ethnographic subjects. No methodological distinction was made between social facts taken from 'exotic' societies and those drawn from Western society. Articles in *Documents* were therefore as likely to be concerned with Hollywood movies, slaughter-houses, popular thrillers or even surrealist painting as the masks of the Dogon or initiation rites among the Bambara.

Seventeen issues of *Documents* were published before it folded in 1931 when Wildenstein withdrew his finance for it, alarmed, according to Leiris, not with its unorthodox nature so much as with the fact that it was losing so much money.

Whether or not Bataille had intended the people around *Documents* to function together as a group, there is no doubt he was soon keen to develop a collective sense within which to work. In 1933, he participated in René Lefeuvre's 'Masses'. This was an attempt to found a popular university, established through the Cercle Communiste Démocratique of which Bataille was a member. As Marina Galetti argues,[20] this was an embryonic form of the later Collège de Sociologie that Bataille would be instrumental in establishing in 1937. The intent behind Masses was to create a forum for discussion of socialist themes in an environment which would bring together workers and intellectuals for a common project. This had become particularly urgent with the rise of fascism and in view of Hitler's accession to power in the same year. 'Masses' responded to a need for an organic movement to address the key issues of the age especially to understand the nature of hierarchy and authoritarian forms, and it also sought to bring the idea of the sacred into the realm of political debate, something that would become particularly important for Bataille in the coming years.

As a project, 'Masses' seems to have barely got off the ground and its activities lasted only for a few months. Nevertheless, the impulse to which it responded was something that was very important for Bataille. This came more to the fore with his collaboration in 1935 with the surrealists in the group Contre-attaque.

Contre-attaque was an anti-popular-front group founded both against fascism and against the perceived sell-out of revolutionary principles by Stalinism. The surrealists had for some time been looking to take part in an alliance of revolutionary intellectuals, and since they had issued their tract 'Appel à la lutte' in 1934, when they called for unity of action among left-wing writers and artists, they had felt an increasing sense of isolation in regard to what they perceived as a betrayal of Marxist revolutionary principles by the Communist International and especially by the French Communist Party, which was completely controlled by people loyal to Moscow.

In 1935, the signing of the Stalin–Laval pact of mutual assistance completed the surrealists' disillusion and they definitively broke with the French Communist Party with their declaration 'On the Time that the Surrealists Were Right' (August 1935). This brought them closer to

Bataille, who had long been on the margins of French communism as a member of Souvarine's circle.

By the summer of 1935, the convergence of the French Communist Party with the ideology of the Popular Front was complete: the workers were urged to abandon the class struggle and sing the 'Internationale' in conjunction with the 'Marseillaise' as the PCF came to advocate everything that signified the end of revolutionary possibilities: the workers were asked to abandon revolutionary defeatism, internationalism and the class struggle and instead give support to 'socialism in one country', national reconciliation, the defence of democracy and the building up of a strong French army.

Bataille's friends were at one with the surrealists in deploring these developments and Contre-attaque was an attempt to build a united front against the tide of the time. Its initial declaration calls for new tactics appropriate for the time to pull society back from the brink of destruction and war. The mood was violent and uncompromising, a contrast to the conciliatory attitude of the communists.

Contre-attaque was a serious attempt to build a political platform against the Popular Front. The trouble was that the participants in the group were largely professional people, academics and intellectuals. It drew few workers or political activists having the organisational ability to hold together such a group. This was compounded by the fact that its two most prominent participants, Bataille and Breton, both had a distaste for qualities of leadership and both of whom sought a kind of 'acephalic' organisation, with the actual organisation largely taking care of itself. However, it seems unlikely that a group committed to political activity and thus to taking an active position in relation to the surge of the age, could have the heterogeneous structure of the Surrealist Group, or Bataille's later Acéphale. Contre-attaque fell between two poles, being neither an intimate circle nor a political party. It seems to have had little impact and seems to have more or less internally disintegrated before the withdrawal of all the surrealists early in 1936 sounded its death knell.

Contre-attaque remains interesting in Bataille's evolution as bearing witness to the tenacity of his desire to found the basis of a community and to involve himself in collective action. It also provides a further development of the way of structuring a group around presentations of material for discussion. From this period Bataille's own text 'Popular front in the street' in particular is an example of the sort of discussion document prepared in the context of Contre-attaque. In this respect, this work very much looks forward to the structure of the College of

Sociology, especially the conference he was to have prepared with André Breton on 'Authority, crowds and chiefs'. This was the aspect of Bataille's work that would gain a more concrete form in the complementary groupings he founded in 1937: Acéphale and the 'College of Sociology'.

The College of Sociology, Bataille's next project, had a more esoteric intent.[21] Its foundation was laid by Bataille in collaboration with Roger Caillois and Jules Monnerot in discussions at the end of 1936 and early 1937. It was very much aimed at an elite of intellectuals, and sought to found 'a moral community, different in part from that ordinarily uniting scholars and bound, precisely, to the virulent character of the realm studied.'[22]

Despite the name, the College of Sociology was affiliated to no educational establishment. It was financed entirely by the members themselves through subscription fees, and its meetings were held in the back room of a Parisian bookshop. What was significant about the College of Sociology in terms of traditional educational research methodology was that it took a position against a scholarship based upon disinterested knowledge, and expressly called for the exploration of a realm that committed its members to the pursuit of interested knowledge. From our discussion of Bataille's dissatisfaction with the way science approached the sacred, we can see what the exigence was to which the College of Sociology directly responded. Where scholars are usually expected to pursue their research without regard to the consequences that may issue from it, the College of Sociology required that those who participated within it should feel under a moral obligation to act upon the results of their research. This was seen as a form of activism that would be defined as a 'sacred sociology'. It was, therefore, to be an attempt to confront the sacred on its own ground.

The structure and methodological approach of the College of Sociology built upon Bataille's experience with *Documents* and *Contre-Attaque*. The founding manifesto of the College of Sociology makes plain its point of departure. It immediately sets itself against traditional science, which

> has been timid and incomplete . . . because science has been too limited to the analysis of so-called primitive societies, while ignoring modern societies, and . . . because the discoveries have not modified the assumptions and attitudes of research as profoundly as might be expected.[23]

The perspective put forward took up Marx's challenge in the *Theses On Feuerbach* that: 'Philosophers have hitherto only *interpreted* the world; the point, however, is to *change* it.' For the College of Sociology, the 'activism' of their sociology would gain a contagious aspect and ally, in good surrealist fashion, the desire to 'change life' with that towards the 'transformation of the world'.

The College was founded at the beginning of 1937 and functioned until the middle of 1939. It met approximately every two weeks and most of the presentations were made by Bataille or Roger Caillois.[24] Reviewing the activities of the College in the last presentation given in June 1939, Bataille claimed that its great merit was to have displayed a 'power to call everything into question'.[25] The common theme of all the lectures was the nature of social cohesion and this was especially central to all of Bataille's own presentations, which generally sought, as he stated, to focus on 'the efforts man has made to discover what he really is, in the absence of unity of person.'[26]

The College of Sociology has been seen as an outgrowth of the Durkheimian school and in a sense it was. Certainly what motivated Bataille's participation was the realisation, taken from a reading of Durkheim, that religion was a motor of society. But this starting point must be seen in relation to the real focus, which was to give a new dimension to Marxism, which had hitherto tended to ignore the communifying motion of society, emphasising social disruption in the form of the inevitability and immediate necessity of a struggle of class against class. As a philosophy of dissolution, Bataille regarded Marxism as incomparable, but it had stopped at dissolution and, tying itself to economic determinism, had neglected to analyse the complementary motion, which determined the way in which social bonds were formed and how society therefore held together. For Bataille a dual movement was involved, so that social dissolution was nullified by this communifying movement, which it was essential to understand. This therefore was the immediate task of a sacred sociology.

How successful was this immediate aim? It is difficult to judge this in as much as we still lack any really concrete information about the activities of the group beyond the content of the actual lectures. Did the members feel a real sense of community, and did the experience serve to give them a focus from which to understand the sacred internally as well as externally? Roger Caillois seems to have later regarded the whole idea as a mistake and to have felt somewhat embarrassed by his own participation in it.

Bataille himself never renounced the impulse behind the College but also seemed to feel a little uncomfortable about it in retrospect. Nevertheless, it should be remembered that the College of Sociology was a perhaps unique attempt to engage with an active scholarship, that would give such scholarship a collective form, and this is something that is not at all negligible.

Parallel to the College of Sociology, Bataille also established an even more enigmatic association, the secret society Acéphale.

Where the College of Sociology had been open of access, and the content of its work is now well documented, Acéphale was a closed 'secret' society, and what happened within its framework remains largely a matter for conjecture. Its genuinely conspiratorial character is beyond doubt and none of the participants has betrayed this character by providing easily accessible details of what happened in this 'voyage to the end of the possibilities of man'. The silence has only been broken by Michel Fardoulis-Lagrange who has spoken at length about Acéphale in language which retains an appropriately conspiratorial and sacred character as it conveys the atmosphere created within its context:

> They sought the lost and still warm track, beyond given signs; and they frowned in the presence of what remained thankless and refractory. To point that each member became executioner and victim. . . . The male element and the female element each flowed into one another and henceforth they preceeded to transgress through their excessive desire as they contemplated the fading breath of a dying man in order to respire and recollect fundamental unity.[27]

The sense of complicity in the collapsing of boundaries was fundamental. The participants seem to have felt they were engaging in a confrontation with the beyond, in which the atmosphere was permeated with something about to happen:

> Mystery had two faces, one turned outside and the other inside, the inside being tumult and chaos, and the outside the surpassing with a view to a new order. The ceremony took place outside while inside only waiting existed. On their own the open eyes made two absolute stains outside as well as inside.[28]

The activity of Acéphale, which perhaps can be usefully compared with the surrealists period of sleeping fits, undoubtedly generated a certain magnetism and intensity which nevertheless caused the participants some disquiet, and not only on account of its disturbing quality. Patrick Waldberg, in the letter to his wife Isabelle, published in *VVV* in 1944, speaks in violent terms about the pretensions of Acéphale (although he was careful to imply no reproach to Bataille), which he said gave him a sense of nausea because of the lack of humour and modesty it displayed.[29]

Following the collapse of both the College and Acéphale and with the coming of the war, Bataille reassessed his focus on the way the sacred functioned in contemporary life. He gave up any direct attempt to found a community and withdrew into himself to explore what he called 'inner experience'. This did not mean he was turning his back on social concerns. If anything the opposite was the case: by a plunge into himself he was affirming how much his reality was inextricably united with that of others. But a displacement was apparent, since Bataille did withdraw from considering the sacred within its collective context to try to comprehend it directly through the experience of the subject, that is himself. His disillusion was with any active aim of seeking freedom: 'Each of us learns with bitterness that to struggle for freedom is first of all to alienate ourselves.'[30] He came to feel that there was an irrevocable contradiction between any striving towards an end and the end itself. The end could never justify the means, since the means used would always determine the ends that could result. What one needed to examine more than anything, therefore, was one's own inner sense in relation to social reality. This is essentially what he meant by 'inner experience'.

Inner experience now provides the contrast with orthodox scholarship and Bataille defined the distinction as being between 'solidity' and 'sovereignty'. Orthodox knowledge founds itself in solidity. But such knowledge is only half complete. He explains:

> If we are to have a learning worthy of the name, which would not be limited to fragmentary outlines, we can relate each object to any other in an indifferent way. But the operation is of value only if one of the terms of the relation occupies in the succession of appearances one or the other of two positions, *solidity* or *sovereignty*.[31]

Bataille is never very clear about how these two types of knowledge respond to each other, but he makes it plain that it is important to differentiate them and not allow one to contaminate the other. What is most important is to keep totality in mind and guard against fragmentation which is the enemy of all coherent thought.

Solidity is traditional scholarship which 'as far as possible draws an object out of dependence on others, so assuring its autonomous subsistence'.[32] The value of solidity is to prevent the object slipping away; it serves to preserve, holding the object in a stable and static relation which denies all dynamism and ambivalence, conserving it as a focus for detached analysis. Sovereignty, on the other hand, refuses to conserve, and founds itself in an unmeasured prodigality.'

It is obvious that Bataille prefers sovereignty, since this is the area in which most of his own work lies. Nevertheless, the operation of solidity remains essential, for without it the sovereign operation would flounder in a closed circle. Bataille does not envisage collapsing this distinction, which remains fundamental. I think it is why he felt uneasy about Heidegger's work. Unlike Mauss or Durkheim, for instance, who were devoted to the work of solidity, Heidegger draws upon sovereignty without being prepared to accept the consequences. For Bataille, the sovereign operation requires placing one's being in question, and by accepting a quiet life and a comfortable university position Heidegger was betraying the possibility of the sovereign operation. Unlike Sade or Nietzsche, unlike Bataille himself, Heidegger was unwilling to place his life in stake through his research. This devalued his claims towards sovereignty. Bataille made the same reproach against Hegel:

> I have trouble concerning that "wisdom" – science is linked to inert existence. Existence is a tumult which overflows, wherein fever and rupture are linked to intoxication. Hegelian collapse, the finished, profane nature of a philosophy whose movement was its principle, stems from the rejection, in Hegel's life, of everything which could seem to be sacred *intoxication*. Not that Hegel was wrong to dismiss the lax concession to which vague minds resorted in his time. But by taking work (discursive thought, project) for existence, he reduces the world to the profane world; he negates the sacred world (communication).[33]

This reliance closes the possibilities unleashed by sovereignty. I think that Bataille believed one had to make a choice between solidity and sovereign knowledge. One could not mingle the two. If one's activity was drawn to solidity then one should accept the disciplinary constraints of traditional scholarship. One had to enter into the research with the recognition that science was unable to answer ultimate questions because it was tied to its own methodological postulates. If one claimed sovereignty, though, one had to be prepared to place one's own being in question.

Sovereignty asserts itself thought its transformative, transgressive impetus. As such it becomes a qualitative realisation of the quantitative findings of solidity. It is in this way that knowledge gains its contagious quality.

Provisionally it may be possible to speak of this activity as being subversive of established practice, but if so it is only in a particular sense. It does not attempt to subvert scholarship but to use it by incorporating its finding within the sphere of a *general economy* which would transform the necessarily restricted nature of such findings into something having a general application. As a critique sovereignty is not directed against established forms. Its methodological focus is quite different but it does serve to focus the essential limits of established forms. For Bataille science is not in need of reform or change, except to the extent that it remains too complacent about its limits, when it remains too timid and too tied up with those limits. When this happens, science tends to become blind to the limits of its applicability and puts forward as a definitive truth what is only a provisional calculation based on the information available within the restricted domain it has set for itself. To go beyond these limits, to transform quantity into quality, a leap into the unknown territory of sovereignty is called for. Bataille expressed sovereignty, then, as being 'a voyage to the end of the possible of man. Anyone may not embark on this voyage, but if he does embark on it, this exposes the negation of authorities, the existing values which limit the possible.'[34]

That Bataille could hardly be said to be hostile to orthodox scholarship is evidenced by the appearance of *Critique*, a new journal he founded and whose first issue appeared in 1946. The quality of *Critique* was immediately recognised and in 1947 it was awarded a prize as the best new journal by the Journalists' Guild. Despite financial difficulties in its early years, *Critique* continued to be published for the rest of Bataille's life and he remained the editor until near the end (the journal itself is in fact still being published today under the editorship of Bataille's friend Jean Piel).

Critique was as carefully (and, if in a different way, as subversively) edited as *Documents*. Its editorial rationale was deceptively simple: it would be limited to articles based around recently published books. There may not seem to be anything radical about such an idea,[35] but Bataille's strength was always the way he chose both material and contributors. The articles that appeared in *Critique* were rarely book reviews: the contributors were encouraged to develop an argument around the book and extend its themes (an invitation that most of them were glad to take up) and the books chosen for review covered were culled from a vast area, drawn, as it states in the introduction to the journal, from the areas of 'literary creation, philosophy and historical, scientific, political and economic knowledge'. The variety and quality of articles published was staggering. In the first year of *Critique* they ranged from Georges Ambrosino on nuclear energy to Maurice Blanchot on Hölderlin, from André Bazin on the history of the cinema to Jean Demarchais on the Political Economy of the USA, from Alexandre Kojève on Christianity and Marxism to Charles Autrand on the future for man after Buchenwald. *Critique* also served a political purpose, defending a position that would preserve the distinct and yet multifarious social critique initiated by surrealism against the fashionable existentialism of the day, which Bataille considered to be a 'sick philosophy of a morose virtuosity'.

As we consider Bataille as a thinker, his novels present us with special problems. Their status is difficult to ascertain. They are certainly not literary excursions, but represent extremely important attempts to grapple with issues that Bataille could not deal with otherwise. They cannot be considered separately from his sociology, and yet at the same time they must be differentiated from it. They are not simply a means to explore the same questions in a different way. And we would be making a serious error if we were simply to treat the novels as having the same status as his other writings. To view them merely as being scandalous would also be a serious error, even if they draw attention to themselves in their 'unacceptable'· qualities. But it is the rubric of transgression rather than scandal that should perhaps be applied. Above all, we need to remain alert to the way Bataille conceived them as having a fundamental transgressive nature, but as always with Bataille, it should be recalled that any transgression has meaning only in relation to the taboo being transgressed. This is perhaps how they should be viewed in relation to his other works: as a transgression, as a shameful, guilty underside to his openly published work. They remain dirty and unacceptable for this reason.

In his lifetime, Bataille published only two novels under his own name, *L'Abbé C* and *Le Bleu du ciel* (translated as *Blue of Noon*)[36], and the latter was published more than twenty years after having been written. *The Story of the Eye* was published clandestinely under the pseudonym 'Lord Auch'; *Madame Edwarda* and *Le Mort* likewise under the pseudonym 'Pierre Angélique', while *Le Petit* appeared under the name 'Louis Trente'.[37] *My Mother* was never published during his lifetime, and it seems that Bataille was trying to work on the text to make its content more 'palatable' for publication. The subject was

something Bataille was extremely sensitive about. When Jules
Monnerot published his article 'Sur Georges Bataille' in 1948, he tells
us that Bataille was furious with him for having revealed him as the
author of *The Story of the Eye* and *Madame Edwarda*. According to
Monnerot, Bataille had a desire for a sort of fictive secrecy, and felt that
Monnerot had betrayed this. He wrote:

> I don't doubt I offended both his rather absurd feeling of
> respectability . . . and also a sense not so much of secrecy, but of the
> fiction of secrecy. There was an element of play. Bataille wanted
> everyone to know that he was the author of both *Inner Experience*
> and *The Story of the Eye* but was drawn to a sort of comedy of
> duplicity.[38]

What were the reasons for this reticence? They are complex and reveal
a great deal about Bataille's personality.

First, he certainly had a sense of 'shame' about these writings. In his
dualist way of thinking, they were documents of transgression that were
both necessary and yet to be refused. They also served as explorations
of different facets of his being: 'When all is said and done,' he once
wrote, 'I have more than one face. I don't know which is laughing at
which.'[39] In all of Bataille's novels the process of dissimulation is
apparent: his characters seem to be hiding behind their names, masking
themselves as they unmask, peeling levels of their personality away
only to reveal other unsuspected elements of deception. Each of the
narratives, indeed, seems to hide the very truth it seems to be revealing.
In this respect, we should perhaps point out an error that Susan Sontag
makes in her essay on 'The Pornographic Imagination'. In a note, she
berates the US publishers of the translation for the fact that they
included only the story of *Madame Edwarda* and not the preface by
Bataille. She states: '*Madame Edwarda* isn't a *récit* padded out with a
preface also by Bataille. It is a two-part invention – essay and *récit* and
one part is almost unintelligible without the other.[40] While Bataille's
preface has certainly become inseparable from the story and the
interrelation is fascinating, it was certainly not conceived in the way
Sontag asserts. The story was first published in 1941 and included no
preface. It was only with the third edition (published in 1957) that
Bataille included his preface (this doubtless explains why the English
language edition did not include it since it was first published in 1956).
However, it is also important to realise that the interrelation between
preface and story is based on the fact that it is a story by 'Pierre
Angélique' prefaced by 'Georges Bataille'. They are not, that is, really

written by the same person; in writing *Madame Edwarda* Bataille was essentially becoming *other* (Marcel Duchamp's play on the character of Rose Sélavy might be an appropriate comparison). One also falsifies Bataille's intention by considering *Madame Edwarda* as an artistic whole, since it is rather the case that preface and story serve to bring each other into question.

In part the use of pseudonyms and false dates of publication may have been stratagems to avoid prosecution. Certainly Bataille would not have liked to have caused a scandal and become a *cause célèbre*, most especially because it would have involved taking a stand. This would have created a dilemma for him since he would have considered it hypocritical to have defended his books on any other grounds than that they were transgressive and unacceptable books, something that would have been no defence at all. There could be no defence for his novels because they were, in his eyes, indefensible. In a sense this has nothing to do with the pornographic content. To assert some high moral ground for any work of art was to negate it, since its value for Bataille could only lie in its sovereign, that is non-assimilable, quality. Literature could never be, in his view, an uplifting experience. As he was to state in *Literature and Evil*: literature is guilty and can only plead guilty.[41]

This in fact appears to be where Bataille perceived the difference between literature and science as lying: science has an innocence, which it maintained through its separation of subject and object. Literature could not offer such an alibi.

The 'truth' of Bataille's novels perhaps resides in the statement made in *L'Abbé C* that the secret of a book lies in the fact that it 'is estimable only when skilfully adorned with the indifference of ruins'. Literature as Bataille conceived it represented a disgust with language. By engaging with it, one was divulging something of the secret of the world. This in itself caused a sense of anguish, for it is through language most especially that man denies his connection with the natural world.

From this perspective, language is culture *par excellence*, and it was necessary, when handling it, to engage with the sense of shame it involved. It is as if to write was for Bataille itself a taboo experience and so the action of writing was transgressive precisely through the process of naming. In his novels, it is this sense of transgression that comes to the fore. His characters affirm their identity by naming experiences that would otherwise be consigned to the void, but this very experience remains ambiguous: 'the only way to atone for the sin of writing is to annihilate what is written.'[42]

Literature could be a sovereign form, but only when it renounces literary effects to become a vehicle of communication. Above all it needed to dispense with any type of rhetoric and become its own realisation, thus releasing the transformative qualities it contained within itself. In so far as it could achieve this, literature could become myth and this is the direction it should be moving.

In accordance with surrealism, then, Bataille saw that literature should return to the land of myth and oppose itself as living truth to the world of fiction in which modern literature is bogged down. As such it should attempt to recover a ritualised context and there should be no separation between author and reader, or between presence and representation. With the different faces that Bataille assumed in his novels he was giving voice to the different aspects not simply of his own internal personality but also of his perceived 'community'. To this extent the characters of Lord Auch, Tropmann, Pierre Angélique and Louis Trente are real; they are not pseudonyms for Bataille.

Bataille's novels function in other ways as a negation of his theoretical work. Where social communion is the central theme of the latter, in the novels the predominant theme is betrayal and the breakdown of communication. Any sense of communion seems impossible. Most of his characters seem to be living under a malediction, a curse that is the predicament of life itself. Their condition is an anxiety in which an inexorable destiny brings them hallucinations and sickness. Treachery and despair are predominant motifs, marking the mood in a relentless way. They represent explorations of laceration and nudity and the physical and emotional vulnerability of the human body and Bataille uses the novel form to engage with these questions in a way that is not possible in his directly theoretical works. Nonetheless, there remains considerable crossover: *The Impossible*, as we mentioned, is both narrative and theoretical text; the final chapter of *Eroticism* is also the preface to *Madame Edwarda*, while the latter story was originally written in conjunction with the 'Torture' section of *Inner Experience*, of which Bataille said it represents the 'lubricious key'.

Bataille's novels point to the existence of another language for the expression of inner experience, one that is freed from any requirement for objective proof, something which even the reflections of *La Somme athéologique* remain tied if only to a slight degree. They respond to a need to open the wound even more, to look horror full in the face and recognise one's identity within the realm of transgression.

In this respect as so many others a strange inversion has take place in the work of Bataille's admirers. Today a philosopher like Derrida engages with philosophy as if he was writing fiction and claims for philosophy the sort of licence traditionally offered to novelists. For Bataille exactly the opposite exigence was at play: he demanded the same rigour for writing novels as for writing philosophy and never sought to subsume the one into the other.

Although there may be a temptation to consider Bataille's novels within the realm of literature, this temptation should be resisted. Rather they need to be considered as the negative underside of his more 'respectable' work, displaying 'another face' that deepens his sociological research. Although his work must be considered as a whole, everything he wrote responds to the social themes that were always his primary concern. Despite the variety of his work, Bataille always remained a social thinker. And this is why it is legitimate to consider him as essentially a sociologist (or, perhaps one might more accurately say, a 'non-sociologist'). His sensibility was not that of a poet (it was even less that of a novelist). He was too absorbed with exploration of social conditions to be able to stand back and metamorphose his experience into poetry. The poetry he wrote has a perfunctory quality: it remains an exploration of the condition of existence (another adjunct, another face, for the exploration of social themes) rather than (and this, as Bataille himself would assert, is the condition of authentic poetry) an attempt at the transformation of that condition. He can only analyse his anguish, he cannot transform it as did, say, his friend René Char, who grappled with a similar sense of anguish and need for social belonging, but whose writings always take language beyond the condition of being to the realm of freedom that is poetry. There is always something that holds Bataille back from any sense of the transformation of being. He sometimes experiences great joy, but seems unable to give expression to it without immediately qualifying it. He recognised this: 'I write like a bird singing as dawn approaches. With (unfortunately!) anguish and nausea bearing down – terrified by dreams of night.'[43] Even the dawn, then, will remain haunted.

This is a definition of Bataille's work that it is important to retain: he is a social thinker of the first importance who utilised different modes of expression to explore different aspects of his own social experience.

Bataille was well aware of his incongruous position. But though he wanted his work to be treated as a whole, he did not want the different elements to be subsumed together. He chose to separate the novels from inner experience, which he conceived in a fundamentally different way to his more directly sociological material. As we should again emphasise, he did not seek to undermine the sciences but to open them up and make them responsive to considerations of material he believed should belong to their domain and yet was too often expelled from their purview. Above all science needed to recognise the need not only for knowledge but also for non-knowledge. Without the latter, knowledge is an enslavement, a meaningless accumulation that destroys the meaning of life. He wrote that he considered that we are 'enslaved by knowledge, that there is a servility fundamental of all knowledge, an acceptance of a mode of life such that each moment has meaning only in terms of another, or of others to follow.'[44] Against this enslavement, knowledge needs to be recognised as what it is: a momentary gleam in the night that fades in the moment it is born. One can only grasp it by perverting its nature. The path to knowledge, then, is impossible. But it is in recognising this impossible quality that the real meaning of knowledge becomes apparent. Its 'impossibility' does not at all diminish it: 'The door must remain open and shut at the same time. What I wanted: profound communication between beings to the exclusion of the links necessary to projects, which discourse forms.'[45] True knowledge needs to recognise its provisional nature and stand against eternal truths. The absolute could only be false and anyone who believed they could reach it was suffering under a dangerous delusion. And while inner experience was not reducible to objective scientific criteria, when it came to more objective scientific research, Bataille nevertheless expected to be judged in terms of traditional methodology, the validity of which he certainly did not at any time deny: 'I am not a scientist, in the sense that what I am talking about is indirect experience, not objective material, but as soon as I talk objectively I do so with the inevitable rigor of the scientist.'[46]

Chapter 5

Expenditure and the general economy

Initial acquaintance with Bataille's work may not incline us to expect him to venture into the realm of economics. In the preface to *The Accursed Share* he displays some irritation at the fact that people were often amazed when he told them he was writing a book on political economy. To the extent that Bataille's approach to economic questions flatly and quite openly contradicts the basis of economic science, one can understand the difficulty of integrating his theories into any sort of conventional economics. Certainly it is not every book on economic theory that defines one of its central arguments as lying in an affirmation that 'the sexual act is in time what the tiger is in space'.[1] Nevertheless, the political economy is central to Bataille's concerns, indeed provides the pivot around which his ideas of the social revolve, and his argument demands to be taken seriously.

To appreciate its importance, we need to understand what he meant by his concept of the general economy, which he put forward as distinct from traditional economics, which he defined as being concerned with the 'restricted economy'. It was also a concept that was connected to the notion of sovereignty and ties in with the interplay between individual needs and the requirements of social interaction.

As sovereignty considers questions of existence in their widest frame of application, so analysis of the general economy must consider economic factors in their totality, taking into account not simply the objective fact of the financial structure of society, but also the social and psychological factors upon which it is founded. In the same way that sovereignty is opposed to solidity, the general economy needs to be seen against the restricted economy, which, in accordance with the standard methodology of the sciences, is based upon a violation of any need to consider the totality of phenomena. As Bataille points out at the beginning of *The Accursed Share*, it is easy to change a tyre, open an abscess or plough a vineyard without taking into account the whole nexus of relations which make such activity possible, since the limited action necessitates only a restricted application. This is analogous with the limited application of science when it legitimately isolates the phenomenon it deals with in a specific case to make an experiment within a restricted field. But for Bataille, as the overall understanding of scientific issues can never be fully understood within such a narrow frame, this must be especially so for the economy because the economy permeates the whole social panorama. As he states:

> economic activity is so far reaching that no one will be surprised if a first question is followed by other, less abstract ones: In overall industrial development, are there not social conflicts and planetary wars? In the global activity of men, in short, are there not causes and effects that will appear only provided that *the general data of the economy* are studied? Will we be able to make ourselves the masters of such a dangerous activity . . . without having grasped its general consequences? Should we not, given the constant development of economic forces, pose the *general* problems that are limited to the movement of energy in the globe?[2]

It was in the domain of economics, therefore, that Bataille saw the operation of sovereignty as being most immediately and fundamentally applicable.

As we have discussed, Bataille conceived society as a social whole. All the elements in a given society respond to that whole and the society can be understood only if one takes into account all the elements within it. He therefore stands against any conception of social being that reduces society to its constituent parts. In this respect, the restricted concept of the economy based upon scarcity and the need for the accumulation of precious resources is particularly reprehensible because it surrenders the possibilities inherent within society to immediately perceived necessities that are often illusory. Basing himself not on economic theory but on anthropological data, he argues that the economy is neither reducible to strictly economic facts nor understandable in terms of economic activity. Rather it responds to all elements within the social body, and it is for this reason that it is only possible to understand the economy by taking psychological and sociological factors in addition to strictly economic facts into account.

Bataille was not an economist and makes no claim to being so. His understanding of economic theory remained limited and he made no attempt to place his argument within the terms of any pre-existing economic argument. This is of little consequence in so far as he could be said to be throwing down a challenge to all economic thinking and his analysis is directed toward the overthrow of economic principles considered in isolation since this inevitably reflects a system of moral values he rejects. It is nevertheless striking that Bataille was developing his theory at exactly the same time that Hayek was establishing the basis of monetarism. While we can assume that they were unaware of each other's work, it is noteworthy that two such completely divergent theories were becoming established in the same period, just as Keynesian theories based upon planning, calculation and social welfare, were becoming dominant.

Curiously Hayek and Bataille agree in their view that the calculation involved in any form of planned economy was sure to fail, as well as in the belief that the market needs to be opened up to allow it to determine its own nature. But Hayek takes a purely economic starting point founded in a psychological determinism, seeing in a free market a means for a more efficient utilitarian based system which responded to man's naturally acquisitive needs, whereas Bataille sees the economy as containing essential psychological and sociological characteristics which respond not to self-interest, but to a principle of pure expenditure and loss. In some ways it might even be said that both of them are advocates of the general economy. But where Hayek subsumes all social activity to strictly economic considerations, leaving no space for anything else, whether social or psychological needs, to intrude, and makes of money the *sine qua non* of all activity, Bataille gives such considerations only a rather tangential role in considerations of how the general economy functions. For Bataille, and anthropological data in general bears this out, it is the circulation of goods and not the money supply that determines the nature of the economy. For monetarists it is of course homogeneous society that is at stake. Socialism and welfarism eat into the hegemony of market forces which therefore stagnate. It is the market, therefore, which needs to be reinforced. Bataille on the other hand is looking towards an entirely different conception of the economy, one that would serve to destroy utilitarian postulates and institute new possibilities of heterogeneity founded in the need to give.

Bataille considered that life is essentially energy that strives to expend itself uselessly. As it founded itself in work, so humanity has needed to control this basic principle of life. It has developed an urge to exist in duration, and so has tried to create a secure environment. From this perspective, classical economics has been based on the assumption that fundamental to human society is the need to protect scarce resources. Bataille questions this assumption by emphasising the importance of useless consumption and the fact that in at least some societies, perhaps even in all societies prior to capitalism, it was the needs of consumption that were considered primary, not those of accumulation. Societies were not primarily structured in order to satisfy the needs of subsistence (although this was an important factor), but through a need to obtain prestige by accumulating a surplus that could be disposed of in a prodigal way.

We first find this idea explored in 'The notion of expenditure', published in *La Critique sociale* in 1933.[3] For a traditional economics based on the principle of scarcity and predicated on the assumption that man makes rational decisions on the basis of the calculation of personal interest, the first question for economists to consider is how to make scarce resources even out in productive activity – the primary need is perceived to lie in the fact that it is necessary to balance the books. The emphasis must therefore be placed on production, which serves to create the wealth that protects these limited resources. Bataille puts a spoke in the wheel of such calculation, which, he asserts, is the result of utilitarian displacement. It is in the nature of things for any given organism to produce more than it needs for its own survival. As such, economic activity is determined not by scarcity but by the need for circulation of the excess wealth produced. From this perspective, Bataille considered such a society of acquisition to be like a father who provides for his son's lodging, clothes, food and harmless recreation, whilst denying him the right to an expenditure that does not serve production. But 'this exclusion is superficial and . . . it no more modifies practical activities than prohibitions limit his son, who indulges in his unavowed pleasures as soon as he is no longer in his father's presence.'[4]

This sort of utility has a malevolent undercurrent to it, which serves to bind the son to the father and ensure his subservience. The son is guaranteed security to the extent that he abides by what his father has in mind for him. But to the extent that he does remain true to this subservience, the son must be untrue to himself, and remains incapable of expressing what he really cares about, which has to be hidden away. As the key to the son's real needs lies in the unavowed pleasures rather than the practical activities his father would consign him to, so the key to the economy, he asserts, lies not in the productive process, but in the surplus that must be expended. And this is not an expenditure that should feed back into the productive process, but one that is excessive and serves no useful purpose, indeed functions in a way to destroy the very productive process itself by exploding its truth. Deprived of such an outlet for its natural generosity, humanity remains in a state of infancy in which it is unable to make its own decisions.

'The notion of expenditure' is a landmark article and explores the possibilities opened up by the basis thus established. The fact of giving was a human fundamental for Bataille and this entailed a need to give completely, even if that loss became destructive. Wealth was not something that man in the depths of his heart strives towards since he knows, deep down, how vain and unsatisfying the accumulation of wealth is. In so far as we do accumulate we do so only in order to expend the surplus we have acquired in a glorious way and for a purpose that satisfies us precisely because it serves no utilitarian purpose. A society that loses the sense of this prodigality and allows, even encourages, its members to accumulate indefinitely and to their own advantage is a sick society, a society that has in effect established constipation as a principle and remains unable to evacuate the surplus energy it has acquired.

Bataille makes a preliminary distinction between distinct elements of the process of consumption. On the one hand he placed the reducible part which is represented by the minimum needed for the immediate conservation of life (i.e. the subsistence necessary for the survival of society). On the other hand there was the wealth that needed to be created precisely for unproductive expenditure. This was the *accursed share* that Bataille would later make the focus of his more detailed discussion of the general economy. The essential is that the former is not more important than the latter. The restricted economy, however, takes account only of the former. By so doing it undercuts human possibilities.

We need at this point to take a closer look at Bataille's idea of the constitution of society, for what is essential to this argument is the relation of individual to society and the way that social solidarity is maintained.

The need people have to express themselves in excessive and useless – and generally, pleasurable – ways can hardly be disputed. And while economists would doubtless not deny it, few would accept the desirability, or the necessity, of taking such activity into consideration when dealing with questions of economic theory. If it is recognised that there is an economy of leisure it is generally assumed to take care of itself and be quite subsidiary to the essential functioning of the economy in general. If anything, the perceived need is to prevent the economy of leisure from entering the frame of the 'real' economy and if there is a problem it is generally seen to lie in how to *control* people's leisure in a way that it does not interfere with the smooth functioning of the economy of work. The need for laziness works against economic calculations and relates to it only to the extent that human beings are physically incapable of being able to work, being able to *produce*, for twenty-four hours each day. But the extent to which people need rest and play is negatively related to the need for work: the economic calculation made is that people need enough rest to make them fit enough to work as hard as possible and produce as much as they can. Even slave-owners had to give their slaves time for recreation, otherwise they would cease to provide the optimum return on the investment made in them as productive entities. The economy of slavery represents capitalism in its extreme form, in which its principle is taken to its logical conclusion. In this extreme form it does not work: it is recognised that slavery is an inefficient labour system since the slave (the epitome of a person reduced to the level of a thing) is incapable of producing to optimum effect. Therefore an economy of leisure has to be recognised to some extent by capitalism, which it offers as a concession. This concession is defined by work – it is not leisure of itself, but as a necessary respite from the rigours of production and which serves to regulate and allow the economy to function to the maximum of its productive capacity. But at the same time, the need for leisure, especially the need for laziness in itself, is perceived as a curse: it drains productive forces and undermines the society of accumulation that capitalism (which is also the society of the restricted economy) inevitably is.

Bataille disputes the very principle behind this argument. In the first place, he denies that a concession of leisure is at all necessary to the smooth functioning of the economy, since the principle of work is inherent in mankind's nature and we necessarily produce more energy than we need for our subsistence. There is no human need to strive to satisfy the needs of scarcity, because they take care of themselves. But more than this, he asserts that leisure, and the expenditure it demands, lies at the heart of the affective economy, and in this perspective any work that simply satisfies accumulation is a perversion of real human needs. Capitalist society, which explicitly bases an economy on scarcity, is thus a perverse society, devoted not to the satisfaction of its own needs, but to the benefit of a particular part of society that controls the productive process.

In the process, the displacement of economic needs from expenditure to accumulation serves to unbalance mankind's inner sensibility. It means that we become shackled to possessions, overcome by a self-imposed enslavement to the world of things, something which also serves to alienate us from our own inner needs.

This is not simply a process that is limited to the individual. There is here no essential difference between individual and society. It is not at all for Bataille a question of the individual's desire for leisure being at odds with the society's need for production. Society as a whole has the same need for leisure and laziness and a healthy society responds to those needs. Not only are individuals within a given society alienated from themselves, therefore; society is also alienated from its own being. This is the consequence, in Bataille's terms, of the reduction to homogeneity. In many ways the effects for society are more serious still than they are for the individual.

Again there arises the problem within traditional economics that, as for other scientific disciplines, society tends to be treated as an abstract thing that stands above and (whether directly or not) regulates the market. Whether economists believe in the principles of free trade and *laissez-faire* or in those of intervention and a planned economy and even if they recognise the need for individual expenditure, they do not leave a space for the expenditure of society as a whole. While individuals may be offered enough leisure to allow them to work efficiently, the same concession is not given to the society itself, which, since it can be treated purely as an abstraction, can be devoted purely and simply to the work principle and has no need of rest.

Given his basic postulate, Bataille regarded this as absurd. Since he considered society to be a living whole, Bataille believed that all societies are built from the emotions of the people who constitute it and if we wished to understand the way a particular society functioned we could not separate it from the way in which the individuals within that society live their lives. Like those individuals, society too suffers from depression and light-headedness, knows fear and despair, exuberance and hope and is subject to the need for laziness, anger and general effusion. It has as much need of non-productive expenditure as individuals themselves. Denied this exuberance in the ordinary course of events it will take an often savage revenge. For Bataille this takes its most deadly form in modern warfare, which represented more clearly than any other social form the need for the expression by society of an expenditure that goes beyond all limits. War is an expenditure that represents the continuation of the economy, in contemporary society, by other means.

In Bataille's view the fact of basing the economy on production was a recent phenomenon that had been introduced into society primarily with the growth of capitalism. He considered that it was not at all apparent that economic interest and the practice of accumulation were inherent to human activity. Rather this was a very late development. In general, societies are based upon the principle of the necessary circulation of resources. In this connection expenditure must be of more importance than accumulation. He found support for this opinion in the data being collected by ethnographers and especially by the theory put forward by Marcel Mauss in his 1925 essay *The Gift*,[5] which was crucial for the development of Bataille's own argument.

In pre-capitalist societies wealth is determined not by what one retains in reserve but by what one squanders. This had persisted through medieval times and had been retained in Catholicism, whose ideology served to legitimate a hierarchical structure of society which remained organised as an organic whole in such a way that bonds of mutual assistance maintained a graduated and static structure. The three principal elements within the society were the clergy, the military aristocracy and the labour force. The labour producers satisfied the needs of the priests and the nobles, in return for which the former offered them spiritual protection, while the latter offered material protection. In such a schema it was the responsibility of the rich to provide for the poor to the extent of ensuring that they did not die from hunger. The failure to do so would threaten the whole social fabric. At the same time, wealth should not be used for the increase of wealth, something which went against fundamental principles of being: usury was forbidden by canon law. Everything in medieval society served the maintenance of a perceived natural order, rationally and morally structured. But at the same time it was a static society that had been given once and for all. No possibility was offered for dynamic change.

The rise of the capitalist class challenged this static equilibrium and ultimately tore it asunder, having gained an ideological justification for acquisition with the rise of Protestantism, which served to break apart the moral authority exercised by the Catholic Church.

In this respect Bataille largely agrees with Weber and with the argument that the convergence of the rise of Protestantism with that of Capitalism was no coincidence. But Bataille also sees the germ of this sensibility as already being present in the fundamental principles of Christianity, even if it was a tendency that had remained latent or had gained only a limited application prior to the Reformation. Nevertheless, the actual principle, which undermined the sacred and has served, historically, to give ideological substance to a principle of utilitarianism, was contained in embryonic form in the very basis of Christianity, even if it took the rebellion of Protestantism to give it an effective form.

The decisive ideological importance of Protestantism in this context was to individualise property and undermine the social basis of the sacred, which had previously served as the social motivation of society and had remained intact in the medieval idea of sovereignty. In giving the individual the right to property, the right to own property, the Protestant spirit also gave the possessor control over his environment and, more importantly, over his wealth. His social role was abrogated. No longer was it necessary for wealth to be fed back into the community, no longer was it perceived as a wealth that belonged rightfully to the whole society and of which the individual possessor was merely a trustee. Now wealth was an individual right whose accumulation was its own justification. Ritual consecration of wealth became obsolete. In so far as wealth needed to be expended, then investment provided the only justification necessary. The primary aim became to use wealth to further augment that same wealth, rather than expend it for its own sake. Expenditure was no longer perceived as something to be undertaken for the common good but was now simply something to serve calculated interests. The organic structuring of society was torn asunder.

Of course, this is not to suggest that previously individuals had not sought to take personal advantage of the system, but its mechanics meant that they were prevented from doing so in an effective way. The conjunction of the rise of Protestantism and a capitalist class eager for a development of productive capabilities, served as the motivation whereby 'primitive economics' (and this means all economic systems before capitalism) was transformed from a concern with expenditure to an obsession with accumulation. It is the whole ideology of the Reformation that provided the moral rationalisation necessary to give accumulation its legitimation. Previously, society was actively structured against individuals assuming power over others or retaining wealth for their own benefit. With the institution of capital accumulation, such activities became the rule. The change of emphasis can be clearly seen in the notion of charity, which is now no longer a communal act of generosity, but becomes something controlled by the individual, who may give or not give voluntarily, but nevertheless to do so now serves not the community but primarily to advance one's own interests. The act of giving is no longer perceived as a necessary gift to the community, but a voluntary dispensation that remains under the control of the person who makes the gift. Equally, no possibility of making a return is inherent in the charitable gift, so that it now serves, in the process of its giving, simply to debase the person who receives it. Capitalism gave this process of gift devaluation its most vital impetus, leading to what Bataille termed, a 'universal meanness'.

As it gave a value to accumulation, so capitalism introduced rational calculation based upon a principle of growth. In the process it broke man's relative equilibrium with the environment and served to estrange us from our sense of ourselves in the world. In the process we became strangers to ourselves and, by the same token, the process began whereby the individual became definitively separated from society. It broke the moral principle that saw usury as an evil and released enterprise from its responsibility to the overall needs of society. Set free in the process from his obligation to the overall good of society, the individual was sanctioned for the first time to accumulate resources beyond immediate personal needs. The intimacy between man and his social environment was broken and we became cast adrift in a world in which value had become displaced. Instead of residing within the activity of people acting for each other it now lies in our relation with things. It is for this reason that Bataille can thus characterise capitalism as an unreserved surrender to things.

Such a society now becomes one in which social distinction is the only measure of one's standing. Servility is established as the principle against which one measures oneself. Where once servility was lost in the general communion of the festival, which consecrated the sovereign unity of society in sacred effusion, so that even though it was hierarchical in nature, society did not make social rank a measure of merit, now social status becomes a mark of a condition of worth which one never escaped. Class distinction gains its rationale and comes to structure the whole of society. Status now determines being rather than, as previously, the other way round. As Bataille put it, 'active impersonality, which requires the *equivalence* of *all* human beings, can never prevail over *distinction*.'[6] Servility therefore permeates every aspect of society, so that power itself is now exercised in servility rather than sovereignty.

This does not mean to say that the need for unproductive expenditure has been overcome. It survives, but in accursed form. The human need expressed in luxury, mourning, war, cults, monuments, games, spectacles, arts and non-reproductive sexual activity remains as great as ever, but everything is done to divert such activity to the needs of utility rather than accept them as the pure effusion they are.

From this perspective, Bataille believed that, in societies which reserve a place for the joyful destruction of accumulated wealth, social cohesion is maintained by ritual forms in a way that prevents the development of class society. Ritual is an active principle, embodied in myth, that affirms the social body and gives to each individual within it a sense of being in which social and individual reality are one.

For Mauss, of course, the purpose of the gift was always to facilitate social relationships. For the economy to function there must be a powerful structure of exchange that covers the whole social domain so that it is not only property and goods that are exchanged but also entertainments, rituals, dance, even women. The purpose of giving is to create a sense of obligation: the person receiving the gift must return it, perhaps with interest. One therefore gives to enhance one's prestige and generosity is society's highest status: someone who never gives would soon become an outcast. In such a way does wealth circulate and if such a system serves to establish social hierarchy it also acts to prevent destructive class conflict.

As he takes up Mauss's analysis, Bataille seems oblivious of what Mauss himself considered the most crucial feature, which was the obligation created by exchange. For Mauss the gift was never a question of pure expenditure without return but quite the opposite. Mauss argued that even the most apparently unconstrained giving was governed by social rules which always required a recompense of equal or greater value. To be sure, Mauss did make it clear that such return could take many forms and the correspondence between what was given and what was returned was never clearly defined. But even so, the gift was not offered out of pure generosity or exuberance: it was part of a complex system of exchange. Bataille is not unaware of this but chooses to disregard it and found his analysis specifically in the act of giving. By doing so, one has to wonder if he was not entirely going against the principle of the argument made by Mauss.

It is true that Mauss was almost as obsessed with exchange as Bataille was with expenditure. It might even be the case that a re-examination of the ethnographic evidence in the light of Bataille's theories could question the extent to which the returning of the gift really had the importance that Mauss ascribed to it. It might well be that expenditure has been underestimated in theories that take a too restrictive view of what constitutes the economy. Let us then examine Bataille's evidence. It has to be said initially that there are certainly problems with Bataille's focus and that as he advances his argument he does so too often by ignoring the postulates of his own argument. The first point we might make here is that while he is very much aware that the basis of the economy lies in providing a store for subsistence, in the absence of which any sort of social solidarity is impossible, too often his analysis ignores this given and proceeds on the basis that it is expenditure in and of itself that determines the nature of the economy, thereby ignoring the role that a preliminary accumulation must play.

In the early part of *The Accursed Share*, for instance, he displaces the issue by recourse to an analogy with the sun, which he claims offers us a gift of its boundless energy without any expectation or even possibility of a return. Clearly in our terms this is so. But if the sun has its own personality and interests (which Bataille's cosmology assumes) then this is something which must necessarily be completely beyond our comprehension. We do not know whether, within the framework of the universe as a whole, the sun is not expounding its energy for some cosmic purpose of its own, a purpose of which we receive an ancillary benefit, but one for which the sun itself has no concern at all.

Equally, it could be said that it is in the sun's nature to expend its energy as it is in ours to receive it. Our nature, therefore, is fundamentally and qualitatively quite different from that of the sun. We exist in relation to the sun and our relation with it is one of absolute dependence. Without its light and warmth our existence would not be possible. The earth does not itself produce any energy independently of the sun, whose bounteous nature is a pre-requisite for earthly existence. Without the sun, the world itself could not even exist as a physical entity. Does this not mean that the nature of the sun is fundamentally different from that of our world? Nothing whatsoever in our existence functions in the way that the sun does. The volcano, another favourite Bataille analogy in relation to expenditure, is not at all benevolent. It does not effortlessly expend its energy so that others may partake of it. In fact it requires a vast accumulation of energy that can no longer be contained before it bursts forth in its abundant and destructive form.

Unlike the sun, the condition of the world's existence is dependence: to sustain itself it needs to receive energy or create it by its own efforts; how it disposes of that energy is a subsidiary problem. In so far as it has an energy reserve, it is only what has been given to it, not what is sovereignly present within it and that it is able to dispense when and how it chooses. Unlike the sun, whose condition *is* energy and which has, so far as we can see, no other purpose than to expend its energy, the condition of the earth is one in which the energy supply is dependent precisely upon the sun's bounty.

From this perspective it seems rather extraordinary that Bataille should explore this issue through a consideration of the society of the Aztecs, a people who appear more than any other to have been aware of the precariousness of the world and were even less convinced of the sun's generosity than we today may be. The whole basis of Aztec society appears founded upon the understanding that the sun did indeed require something to be given back to it in return for its gift, in default of which it would withdraw the favours it offered.

The designation of the meaning of ritual is always a hazardous occupation, and the more so in respect of ceremonies we generally only know through often tendentiously mediated accounts dating back four centuries. Nevertheless, it seems likely that Aztec sacrifice was an untypical form whose extreme nature derived not so much from an inner need for expenditure in itself as from an overwhelming need to expiate a direct sense of guilt and allay an overwhelming fear of retribution.

Bataille sees in Aztec ritual sacrifice, which is devoted to the sun, a movement of expenditure that is comparable to the sun's generosity. It is, however, only fair to point out that elsewhere Bataille himself equates expenditure specifically with guilt and so brings his own argument on this point into some doubt. For now, though, we need to concentrate on the issue of expenditure. First, let us bring Bataille's understanding of Aztec society into focus.

By their own account, the Aztecs found themselves almost by default the most powerful people in what was one of the most culturally rich and variegated areas of the world at the time, since it was chance that led them to build their settlement, which become the fabulous city of Tenochtitlan, on an island that would prove to be an almost impregnable base for expansion against their neighbours. But the Aztecs appear at once overcome with a sense of their own destiny and overwhelmed by the sense of history they saw all around them – the vast monuments and Teotihuacan pyramids, and the myths of the vanished Toltecs preyed on their sense of insecurity. Their own audacity at laying claim to such a heritage seems to have overwhelmed them and they expected that the wrath of these ancient peoples would fall upon them at any time. It was this that led to their prodigality, not an overwhelming urge towards expenditure for its own sake. It may very well be that the excess of Aztec sacrificial forms reveals to us the extreme that a people can go to preserve their sense of social cohesion, but to thereby assert as Bataille does that they are fearlessly confronting the nature of existence by looking death full in the face by means of indulging in a vast hecatomb seems unsupported by the evidence. Quite the contrary, the Aztecs appear to have been a fearful people who indulged in excessive sacrifice to appease not confront hidden forces. Sacrifice for them appears to have been more a means by which to expel rather than confront death. In this respect, and to use Bataille's terms, it would seem more appropriate to consider them a people of servitude than of sovereignty. Aztec sacrifice is unusual in being almost entirely devoted to human sacrifice – neither animals nor victuals were generally sacrificed.[7] Furthermore, the human victims did not come from within the community. They were generally either prisoners of war or very young children who had not yet undergone the ritual that would have introduced them into society. Therefore they did not yet exist as members of Aztec society. This suggests that the sacrificial object had to be something that remained ambiguously both part of the society and yet excluded from it. What was sacrificed was not a natural surplus that had built up and had to be expended. It was a surplus that had been created expressly to be expended. Great efforts were made to raise this surplus to the level necessary to make the prodigious quality of Aztec sacrifice possible. But the Aztec community was sacrificing nothing of itself. Rather, the form of Aztec sacrifice appears to have responded to a need for a surrogate victim to stand in for the community. Sacrifice was performed not only to ensure the survival of society but also, in a sense, of each individual warrior. What is significant is that all the elaborate preparations that each sacrificial victim underwent seem to have been designed to transform the victim into a facsimile of the warrior whose prisoner he was; it is as if he became a double, assuming the characteristics of an Aztec warrior. In this way it seems that the Aztecs were hoping to outwit death by making an offering of themselves in a different form: in sacrifice the warrior died and yet remained alive.

One has to wonder, in fact, if Aztec sacrifice did not serve precisely a homogenising process within their given society. As such it might be considered, contrary to what Bataille believed, to be an example of sacrifice being turned against itself and gaining a profane quality, and its purpose may have been to bind together the homogenous elements of Aztec society in a conclusive way, so serving the taboo. This does not necessarily go against the generality of Bataille's perceptions, but does serve to displace them. In fact, among the Aztecs, the heterogeneous bond of society, based as Bataille believed in excess and transgression, appears to have been centred not around sacrifice but around the communal meal (sundered from a direct connection with sacrifice) which appears to have functioned far more clearly as the heart of the Aztec social world.

In his book on Aztec sacrifice, Christian Duverger has devoted a short section specifically to Bataille's idea of the 'accursed share', making some of these points and emphasising the extent to which Bataille fundamentally misunderstood the nature of Aztec society. This is not because of new ethnographic findings revealed by research since Bataille was writing. There was nothing excessive about Aztec sacrifice. All the ethnographic evidence, from the time of the Conquest, refutes such a suggestion. What most shocked the Conquistadors was not at all the excessive character of what they witnessed, but the opposite: sacrifice was performed as an everyday, inconsequential act. It was something that was taken for granted and subject to little ritual excess. Aztec society was in fact extremely well-ordered and puritan and the human sacrifice performed conformed to this general sense of order. There was no excess, no disordered celebration or sense of intoxication. The cruelty, licentiousness and exuberance that Bataille saw as being its characteristics were entirely absent. The actuality of Aztec society bears little relation to this conception, which is fundamentally a vulgar popularisation fuelled by his own wish fulfilment. It does not necessarily follow, though, that this misunderstanding brings into question Bataille's overall analysis since the argument he puts forward does not rely on this evidence. If in specific terms Duverger is doubtless correct, there are other aspects of Bataille's understanding of the nature of Aztec society that call for further comment. Before taking this further, however, let us consider Bataille's treatment of his other main ethnographic source, which is the institution of the potlatch among the societies of the Canadian North West.

The potlatch ceremony of the North-west Coast American Indians provided Mauss with some of his most dramatic data for analysis of the notion of the gift. The institution of the potlatch is one of the clearest proofs we have of the falsity of the proposition that economic life is determined by self-interest. It serves to clarify the nature of primitive economics and establish the principle that is now generally accepted in anthropological, if not economic, theory, that it was the gift and not trade and barter that is at the root of primitive economics. Trade is a later imposition, arising from what may have been a complementary or even quite different means of economic transaction to which people were hostile and resistant. As a rule, primitive economics precluded trade and considered the idea of bargaining as anathema. Everything suggests that barter is not a primitive form of trade.

If we have cast doubt on the idea of Aztec sacrifice as an expression of excess, there certainly are in the potlatch excessive elements which

Bataille emphasises. However, the ethnographic evidence is by no means clear cut about how important such elements were in the overall significance of the potlatch. Certainly it seems unlikely in the least that the potlatch established a principle of an economy of expenditure and waste. On the contrary, everything suggests that the economy of the potlatch, like all 'primitive economies' represented an extremely efficient use of resources in which waste was anathema. The most complex form of the potlatch, that of the Kwaikiutl, was certainly not performed for the purposes of the destruction of wealth, but for its maintenance and distribution. In so far as it contained excessive elements these were incidental. The purpose of the potlatch was not to serve an excessive movement but the harmony of the society even if it responded to conditions in which over-abundance may have been a feature. If the potlatch did at times assume an excessive form of violence and destruction, this seems to have occurred not because it had a structural purpose but because it was a surplus element latent in the structure.

If Bataille's use of ethnographic data is often unsure, this does not bring his central argument into question. The view that the real needs of the economy lie in expenditure rather than production retains its force. However, Christian Duverger does raise one point that initially might incline us to feel that it fatally undermines an important component of Bataille's argument. Duverger points out that far from functioning as a means of social solidarity, Aztec sacrifice was tied to imperial expansion:

> Human sacrifice is not for the Aztecs a mystical act by which society made its proper oblation for the salvation of the rest of mankind, but on the contrary a technical means of domination which assured the growth of the group at expense of the peripheral populations. Those sacrificed had to be foreign to the Mexican empire in order that the war necessary for their capture could, at the same time, serve to extend Aztec power.[8]

Given this, how can we accept Bataille's contention that 'Sacrifice is the antithesis of production, which is accomplished with a view to the future; it is a consumption that is concerned only with the moment'[9]?

We can take this point further, and give support to Bataille's perceptions, even if slightly displaced, by considering the discussion Tzvetan Todorov has devoted to Aztec sacrifice, which he has very revealingly compared with the brutality of the Spanish during the conquest.[10] Todorov made a distinction between Aztec and

Conquistador violence in terms that have a direct bearing on the nature of the respective societies. He argues that the Aztecs can be considered as representing societies of sacrifice whereas the Conquistadors were the representatives of a newly inaugurated 'society of massacre'.

Todorov's distinction turns on the nature of social cohesion and is very much in line with Bataille's argument. On this point we should also point out that Duverger, in the quotation given above, misrepresents Bataille's understanding of sacrifice on one vital point, that is by imputing to Bataille the view that sacrifice is made for the salvation of mankind. For Bataille it is nothing of the kind and in fact he would consider such an idea as being part of the Christian displacement of sacrifice. For Bataille sacrifice was the opposite of salvation and served the social solidarity of the immediate group, not of mankind in its generality. Its aim was to protect the instant. But Duverger does bring Bataille's argument into question by suggesting that sacrifice serves imperial expansion. If this is so, then sacrifice does not serve the needs of the instant but is a feature of a society that has abandoned sovereignty. Is this, however, the case?

As he discusses the specificity of Aztec sacrifice, Todorov notes that it was characterised by its openness: no attempt was made to hide it from view, it was not something shameful and no attempt was made at dissemblance. It was also determined by strict rules – the victim must be alien, but not too alien. While he must not be an Aztec, he must belong to a neighbouring tribe, that is to a people with whom one has intimate dealings. The sacrifice of a stranger from far away would immediately be vitiated; it would, in fact not be a sacrifice at all. Performed in public and in full view of all, sacrifice testifies to the strength of the social fabric and only takes place within societies which are founded around intimacy and heterogeneity.

Massacre, on the other hand, is the characteristic of societies which have a weak social fabric and consequently tend to reduce themselves to homogeneity. Instead of being placed at the heart of society, violence is now hidden away. Its principle was established by the example of the Conquistadors, who massacred their way across America with a cruelty and violence and in such an abundance that it puts Aztec sacrifice to shame.

Spain in the fifteenth century was a society on the verge of massive imperial expansion, and through such an imperialism the residue of internal violence which sacrifice carries away in a society that still practices its ritual form is now definitively expelled from the heart of the host society. Excessive violence is now performed surreptitiously and in a form that can never be acknowledged. No longer is the sacrifice a form of intimacy involving the relations between one's own and one's neighbouring societies. Now, 'the more remote and alien the victims, the better: they are exterminated without remorse, more or less identified with animals.'[11] The victim can no longer be assimilated into society and made as an extravagant offering, but must become anonymous. To identify the victim would be to make the act criminal; it would become murder and therefore unacceptable. It must be as if it had never existed, as if such violence could not exist. In the process any sacred quality attaching to the act of sacrifice vanishes: massacre is the very denial of the intimacy that sacrifice embodied. What happens is that far away from one's own land, far from the laws of central government,

> all prohibitions give way, the social link, already loosened, snaps, revealing not a primitive nature, the beast sleeping in each of us, but a modern being, one with a great future, in fact, restrained by no morality and inflicting death because and when he pleases.[12]

In this respect the Conquistadors initiated the modern attitude, which seeks to reduce all transgressive violence to the same status, imposing homogeneity in the very process as it weakens the social cohesion within the given society.

Todorov's analysis merges with Bataille's and allows us to see how pertinent Bataille's work remains even if his overall understanding of Aztec society may have been faulty. For we can see here a very clear distinction between the expansionism of the Aztecs, which was not done for territorial gain but to strengthen the centre and maintain its social cohesion, and the imperialism of Spain, which was a response to the breakdown of social cohesion in a feudal society. The Aztecs did not go in search of riches or to subjugate the native populations to themselves but sought the wealth (that is sacrificial victims) that could be expended in excessive violence (in so far as all violence is excessive) that would ensure the fecundity of their society and so ensure their own daily survival. In this sense Aztec sacrifice does retain its sacred quality and remains at the antipodes of production. It stands against the spirit of conquest embodied by Spain. In all probability sacrifice never involved cruelty and degradation; on the contrary the sacrificial victim was an honoured guest. Even in the extreme form that Aztec society gave to it, sacrifice retains its element of communication. In this sense sacrifice can be seen, as Bataille contends, as the experience of self-sufficient societies that cohere in a heterogeneous way. With the inauguration of massacre, however, cruelty and degradation become everyday norms: it is the consequence of the determination to reduce everything to utilitarian value, to reduce the world to the nature of a thing. The modern attitude is defined here and Bataille has made a vital contri- bution to understanding its dark nature. On this point therefore we must question Duverger's criticism of Bataille and contend that Bataille's analysis of Aztec society remains very pertinent

The question that remains, though, is the extent to which primitive economics embodied a principle of pure waste. At this point we might even turn Bataille's argument on its head and suggest that it is modern industrial societies that operate on a principle of waste and expenditure. We do, after all, tend to call the society in which we live a *consumer* society and in Britain we have become used, in a period of recession, to hearing how expenditure was necessary if the economy was to recover. In such conditions expenditure is probably more of a problem that it ever was for the Kwaikiutl.

The problem his argument raises and an issue he skirted around is that if the chemical principle that an organism produces more energy than it requires for its subsistence is true, then there remains the question of how this energy is generated and maintained. It is not spontaneously produced out of nothing. It emerges from the inner drives of the organism. As human beings, then, is it not precisely because we have an inner need for work that our energy surplus is created? If we were to renounce work should we not cease to produce the energy required for survival and simply wither away? It is difficult to see how the energy a human being requires for its existence can be generated if the work principle is renounced altogether and, as we shall see in the next chapter, Bataille's argument about eroticism is based on the fact that work is indeed what determines our being and without which we should flounder. This remains a serious inconsistency in Bataille's work as a whole that is difficult to reconcile.

In this perspective Bataille's concept of class struggle also seems defective. If his model of abundance was accurate and our surplus energy was generated naturally inside us, then those people Bataille saw as being part of the heterology of contemporary society, (those who exist at the lowest levels of society, those whose lives lack the essentials to feed and clothe themselves, those outsiders who are too proud and intractable to knuckle down to everyday demands) would not only be likely to rebel, they would be unable to prevent themselves from rising up spontaneously against their condition. Yet the fact is that the people at the lowest levels of society who are denied the possibilities of work, those who have accumulated nothing, are those who are least likely to rise up against their condition. They have no excess energy to expend because all the energy they have is spent in daily survival and nothing is left over with which to rebel against their condition. Their excess has been appropriated from them, one might say, through the denial of their possibilities through work. Even if the condition of life as a whole, therefore, may be prodigality, it is not something that is necessarily inherent in all existence equally. On the contrary, the surplus and its expenditure may be a luxury of accumulation. If the poor rebel they generally do so in a rebellion which begins with the working classes whose level of accumulation is enough to give them the luxury of expenditure. It may be true that 'those who have nothing' will give such a rebellion its most desperate and excessive forms, but this is only because they have been able to partake of an expenditure delivered up to them by the rebellion of those who have attained a wealth they can afford to expend. This of course is the whole basis of Marx's understanding of class struggle: the proletariat gain a class consciousness that universalises their struggle into a revolt of all people. For Marx, the lumpenproletariat had no revolutionary potential. Can one then have sumptuous expenditure without accumulating resources in the first place? Is there not an inseparable relation between the two and if expenditure is a human necessity it is so only through the prior need to accumulate. The latter can never override the former: we do not destroy more than we have first created and even if we do indulge in ruinous expenditure it is in response to accumulation. It is not a taste for excess that causes a gambler to ruin himself – no one ever gambles in order to lose. It is true that a gambler may become so entangled in the game that he is carried along in an excessive movement to the extent that he would prefer to lose than to stop playing. But even then the overriding desire is to win.

Perhaps it is churlish to dwell overmuch on the faults in Bataille's use of objective data. The criticisms we have made do not serve to undermine the kernel of his theory: they tend to show simply that he lacked the rigorous analytic qualities that made Marx's analysis so devastating in its sphere. If we have been rather critical of Bataille in this respect, it has been necessary to subject his analysis to close examination to protect what is essential about it. Bataille's use of ethnographic sources may sometimes serve to confuse rather than clarify his argument. However, he is certainly on a surer footing when he takes his data from contemporary reality and from historical sources. To redress the balance and show how cogent Bataille's analysis could be, let us take a look at his fascinating analysis of the Marshall Plan.

The Marshall Plan was unveiled by the United States in 1947 in the wake of the devastation brought to Europe by the Second World War. In its aims the Marshall Plan served to focus Bataille's contentions because it was presented as an act of generosity by the United States to revitalise Europe without any expectation of an economic return for itself.

It was not, however, simply the destruction of the war that accounted for the US generosity. What was determining was the threat from Soviet expansionism. The two factors together (European economic chaos and Soviet political ambitions) had made the market economy untenable. According to Bataille the choice was between, 'the silence of communism universally imposed by concentration camps, and . . . *freedom* exterminating the communists'.[13] The war that could result was far from Marx's vision of the transformation of capitalism, but could only destroy it and install a universal darkness.

Nevertheless, this menace had its positive side. It forced an 'awakening of the mind':[14] with the world on a knife edge, any petty calculation of interests became counter-productive and forced the American capitalists to abandon the restricted economy and take the general economy into account. No other course was open to them since to have continued to apply the logic of a market economy would have made it 'impossible for a ruined Europe to return to a viable political economy'.[15]

The Marshall Plan was therefore not an altruistic act by the United States, but was significant in that it placed the long-term interests of the world above those of capitalism and even, possibly, of those of the US itself, since it was impossible to calculate what the effects of the Marshall Plan would be – it might serve to re-vitalise Europe at the expense of the United States. Everything would be done to prevent this from happening, of course, and the ultimate aim was to strengthen the economy of the United States. But this desired consequence could not be calculated beforehand; it was a risk that the peril of the age made necessary.

For the threat that had emerged was not simply an external one from the Soviet Union, but was also revealed internally. This was in the very fact of the level of over-production within the United States economy. Because of the war no one could compete with the States, whose economy had expanded to an extent that was explosive, with no market for the surplus that had been created. Unless such a market could be created out of nothing there would be inevitable war since 'the American economy is in fact the greatest explosive mass the world has ever known'.[16] This meant that it was hard to imagine that the United States could prosper without 'a hecatomb of riches, in the form of airplanes, bombs and other military equipment, [but] one can conceive of an equivalent hecatomb devoted to non-lethal works'.[17] In such circumstances, capitalism needed to renounce its founding principles and expend with no guarantee of profit. It needed, that is, a useless expenditure, precisely this 'hecatomb devoted to non-lethal work'. Admittedly this only came about because of an extreme situation.

The reservations we have made, many of which Bataille was conscious of even if he did not confront their implications, do not undermine the essential elements of his theory of general economy. He is undoubtedly right to focus on the problem of surplus value and the necessity for expenditure, but it needs to be emphasised that expenditure has meaning only in relation to accumulation. Bataille's problems arise when he departs from his own principles and isolates expenditure from the entirety of social relations. Even accepting that we should consider the demands of a general rather than restricted economy as legitimate, it is difficult to see how any conception of a general economy can have analytic value unless it treats the problems of accumulation and expenditure as being inextricably linked. It is impossible to separate one from the other. Indeed, can it not be said that to focus on expenditure at the expense of accumulation merely means that the restricted economy has been displaced from a concentration on accumulation to a concentration on expenditure? The general economy can only take shape if it tackles the relation between the two.

In so far as surplus value presents a serious problem for society, it is equally difficult to see how this can be tackled without taking work into account. If it is the case that a surplus energy is naturally generated within us, then how does this occur? Bataille leaves this issue hanging in the air, assuming that it is simply a natural process. But is it not the case that the production of energy requires the intervention of the will into the being that produces the surplus? Does not a creature that has lost the will to live simply cease to produce the energy it requires for its subsistence? If this is so, then what is the generative force that is responsible for the human energy that creates the surplus? Is it not precisely because we have an inner need for work that we are able to satisfy more than our own energy needs and that, deprived of this urge, we should immediately cease to produce the energy we need for our survival? Is it not, then, urgent to engage with the nature of our will to work before we can seriously consider the importance of expenditure?

It is interesting here to consider the work of Norman O. Brown,[18] since Brown approaches these problems from a perspective very close to Bataille's but develops his arguments with a firmer and more cogent and consistent use of psychological and anthropological data.

Like Bataille, Brown takes Mauss's notion of the gift as his starting point. But where Bataille displaces Mauss's argument from a concern with exchange to one which causes expenditure to become fundamental without questioning Mauss's underlying framework, Brown takes a critical approach to Mauss's work. What Mauss saw as the central question in a consideration of gift exchange was what obligated the person receiving the gift to return it. For Brown this was a secondary question. The important question to be raised was why the gift was made in the first place.

Brown also sees the key to the economy as lying in social relationships and not in the needs of the market. He likewise recognises that the focus for economic activity lies not in a need to engage in trade with a view to self-interest, but in order to facilitate social relationships, safeguard social standing and provide for a generalised distribution of wealth. The rule of economic activity lies not in the exchange, but in the act of giving.

Brown also concurs with Bataille in regarding the need to give as providing the basis for social solidarity: 'Archaic man gives because he wants to lose; the psychology is not egoist but self-sacrificial . . . '[19] The need to give structures the whole of social life and religion provides the frame by which the *raison d'être* for sacrifice is given an objective form in the creation of gods which, according to Brown, 'exist to receive goods, that is to say sacrifices; the gods exist in order to structure the human need for self-sacrifice'.[20] It is for this reason that it is reciprocally necessary to create a surplus.

Equally, Brown agrees with Bataille that it is guilt that provides the basis for the need to give, which is equally tied in with neurosis and excretion. To this extent Brown is in accord with Freud who considered human guilt to be based in a primal crime which can be mitigated only through social solidarity and this accounts for the logic of the communal meal. But he departs from Freud in not accepting the primal crime as an actual event which, reproduced in every generation, becomes biological fact. For Brown the primal crime is an infantile fantasy created by the child as a brake on the excessive vitality (the id) which it is unable to control. Sexual organisation is therefore constructed by the infantile ego to repress bodily vitality. We therefore face the difficulty of overcoming this primal repression. This we can do only if we first of all recognise its neurotic character. This would enable us to 'enter the kingdom of enjoyment'.[21]

Brown's argument is clearly very much in accord with Bataille's, and adds to it much precision (although Bataille would no doubt remain highly dubious about any possible transcendence from the neurotic condition to a realm of enjoyment). Brown's analysis introduces a psychological focus which gives to the argument established by Bataille a more profound aspect. However, there is one point at which Bataille's analysis also serves to add an element to Brown's analysis and this concerns the question of guilt and its incorporation into human psychology. Brown locates guilt as an infantile fantasy that serves to place a brake on instinctual responses defined by the id. This may well be so, but why does such a need arise? Brown simply ascribes it to neurosis, but even if we accept this, it still leaves open the question of how such a neurosis has come to shape human destiny. A neurosis surely must have a cause – it cannot emerge from out of nothing. In failing to investigate this, Brown's analysis remains incomplete and he can do no more than put forward the possibility of future liberation lying in a psychoanalytic cure once the neurotic form was recognised: mankind needs, one assumes, to undergo psychoanalysis. Bataille on the other hand is very clear about where such a primary need for repression arises: it is a manifestation of mankind's guilt at separating itself from nature and assuming a mastery over it by means of work. If this is neurotic, it is still essential to our sense of ourselves as human beings.

This sense of guilt lies in an elementary alienation, which has been accentuated with the development of the complexity of society.

Bearing this in mind, it will be seen that the critiques advanced both by Brown and by Bataille add a powerful element to the Marxist theory of alienation and perhaps need to be considered also in this perspective. Marx's formulation of alienation is worth recalling here:

> Estranged labour not only (1) estranges nature from man and (2) estranges man from himself, from his own active function, from his vital activity; because of this it also estranges man from his *species*. It turns his *species-life* into a means for his life . . . . The animal is immediately one with its life activity. It is not distinct from that

activity; it *is* that activity. Man makes his life activity itself an object of his will and consciousness . . . (3) estranged labour therefore turns *man's species-being* – both nature and his intellectual species-being – into a being *alien* to him and a *means* of his *individual existence*. It estranges man from his own body, from nature as it exists outside him, from his spiritual essence, his human essence. (4) An immediate consequence . . . is the *estrangement of man from man*. In general, the proposition that man is estranged from his species-being means that each man is estranged from the others and that all are estranged from man's essence.[22]

It is valuable to recall this quotation here, since, although Bataille had probably not read this text (which was published for the first time only in 1932), it encapsulates very clearly his starting point and shows why he felt the general economy and the issue of expenditure were of such importance. Like Marx, Bataille considers that all alienation is self-alienation and that the root causes lie deep in the human psyche.

In Bataille's view it was not only individuals who were alienated, it was also the society itself that was alienated from itself. This brings us back to the concepts of homogeneity and heterogeneity. For if there may be an impulse of society to try to establish itself as a coherent entity, in general such cohesion is guaranteed by heterogeneity. In capitalism, though, homogeneity had reached the point of overwhelming every aspect of life. Sacred forms like festival, play and sacrifice can no longer be integrated into the narrow confines of the social structure, which does all it can to reduce everything to the same level.

In capitalism the impetus is to reduce the whole of society to homogeneity. As such, according to Bataille, capitalism represents 'an unreserved surrender to *things*, heedless of consequences and seeing nothing beyond them'.[23]

Heterogeneity therefore becomes a subversive form within capitalist society, and Bataille reproaches socialism for having failed to take this force into consideration. The tie up between homogeneity and alienation is an important aspect of Bataille's work concretised in the fact that the overcoming of alienation can only be achieved by engaging with new possibilities of heterogeneity. This meant a confrontation of one's own alienated self: in the process of overcoming alienation one would need to struggle against the homogenising element imposed by capitalism. If one's own alienation was to be transformed then this would require a simultaneous transformation of society.

For Marx, alienation could be transcended only when 'individuals

reproduce themselves as individuals, but as social individuals'.[24]
Bataille saw this as the crux of the problem; the re-creation of heterogeneity begins when we no longer perceive a distinction between our
own desires and those of society.

Here Bataille's argument is tied in again with Hegel's master and
slave dialectic. However he refused to accept Hegel's contention that
the slave could obtain liberation through work, since work was the
condition of his enslavement. The only way for the slave to obtain his
freedom was to refuse work and engage freely in non-servile,
heterogeneous activity. In this way, Bataille maintains that the
proletariat can liberate themselves only by rejecting their status as
workers. In so doing they assert their universality. Clearly this also
refutes Marx, since for the latter it was work that made the proletariat
the universal class. On this point, too, it is again difficult to see how it
can be made compatible with Bataille's own analysis of eroticism.
Furthermore, in rejecting work (which is surely man's universal
experience), could the proletariat still be seen as a universal class?

Bataille has the problem of extricating himself from the complexity
of Hegel's logic, something which is far more difficult than he thinks.
We will discuss this issue more fully in the next chapter.

If it is necessary for individuals to conceive themselves as social
individuals, then this remains impossible within the structure of
capitalist society. Capitalism is inherently based on individual
enterprise and thus it remains impossible for individuals to reproduce
themselves other than as isolated individuals. The aim of socialism
should therefore be to resolve the conflict between individual and
society so that the individual conceived his destiny both in terms of his
own interests and in the interests of society as a whole (that is, would
cease to differentiate between the two). In practice, though, both
Stalinism and Social Democracy went in the opposite direction, reifying
society above the individual so that alienation became even further
entrenched. Society was now equated with state domination and
established as an impersonal body that stood above people's everyday
needs, but acting in a way so as to both demand onerous duties of
individuals while providing them with basic welfare in an impersonal
way, which is never to be questioned and with which the individual no
longer has any sense of belonging.

Bataille perceived this basic failure within socialism very early in the
thirties. He saw that by failing to address the importance of mankind's
drives and need for a sense of social belonging, socialism had left the

way open for fascism, which responded precisely to the lost domain of social solidarity that not only had socialism singularly failed to resolve, but for the most part it had not even placed on the agenda. Bataille saw that fascism had stepped into this breach left open by socialism's failure to use the deep felt need for social solidarity in order to found itself in a reactionary return to forms of social hierarchy through which the sovereignty lost with the triumph of capitalism could be regained. Fascism relied on a rigidly stratified social structure which would recreate the organic model of the feudal age in a new form. It would correspondingly give back to society values of hierarchy. This was based upon a false proposition, and fascism is doomed to exhaust itself in its initial movement. Nevertheless, it remains of interest as an attempt to recreate heterogeneous social forms in which the complementary needs for stability and expenditure would again be addressed.

Fascism is a perverted and nostalgic form, but it responds to a deep yearning for a meaningful experience of the sacred. And so, for Bataille the success of fascism raised issues that socialism had to address. For the real failure of socialism was that it had opposed capitalism in the domain of its strength, that is in terms of economic utility. Fascism on the other hand had identified the achilles heel of capitalism and its success showed that capitalism had to be confronted in its social forms, not in terms of its economic insufficiency. What was needed, for Bataille, was the development of a sacred of the left hand that would counter the sacred of the right hand that fascism invoked. More than half a century later, this is a question that has barely even been delineated and there seems little denying that Bataille's perception was acute: we can see that only fascism has ever managed to overthrow a capitalist government and no socialist movement has come close to doing so since 1922.

Bataille's analysis of the general economy allows us to see how the practice of socialism has failed to challenge bourgeois values at a fundamental level. In economic terms it has merely displaced the framework of capital accumulation and utilitarianism. This has had disastrous consequences. The very basis of the capitalist economy lies in its dynamic nature, which enables the mechanism of the economy to utilise accumulation in a way that serves as a stimulus to the desire for an expenditure that feeds back into the productive process. But this is something created by capitalism. Such desires have no real basis; capitalism has constructed them for its own reproduction. Socialism, however, has mistakenly taken the desires created by capitalism – which really ought to belong to the ideological realm of appearance and are therefore incapable of being in any way satisfied – as real desires and has striven to satisfy those illusory desires in a more human way than is possible in the cut-throat world of capitalism. But in the process the dynamic of capitalism – founded in individual initiative – is undermined so that a 'socialist' society established on such a basis can only stagnate. It remains unable to either negate or to satisfy capitalism's illusory desires and is trapped in limbo. Either way the result can only be dissatisfaction and degeneration.

The actual logic of the economy itself nevertheless works against the homogenising tendency of capitalism. Since heterogeneity cannot be accommodated within the society, the surplus energy that is still generated by heterogeneous needs must be expended externally. It is this that leads to imperialistic wars and destructive violence.

From this perspective, capitalism does not escape the need for wasteful expenditure, but, through its refusal to acknowledge the need for it, turns it into an accursed form. Instead of the sacred being devoted to life-enhancement as it is in a heterogeneous society, it now assumes uncontrollable and potentially catastrophic forms in the shape of conflict of interest, global warfare, massacres, pollution and nuclear explosion. For Bataille this process is inherent to capitalism and cannot be reformed.

Bataille does not write as a political economist. In advancing his critique, he does not advocate that the restricted economy should take account of the general economy, because by definition it cannot do so. At least, an economy based upon the concerns of the restricted economy is incapable of handling the implications raised by the general economy. His whole analysis is offered as an assault on the primacy of the utilitarian aims that sustain the idea of the restricted economy, the impulse of which has served to lead humanity into an impasse. With *The Accursed Share* he is, in common with all of his other books, issuing a challenge. It would equally be an error to view his argument as an attempt to integrate excess into an economy of calculated ends. The emphasis is upon the destruction of ends in general. He felt that it was essential for us to go beyond such calculation and look towards the possibility of establishing the basis of an economy which would respond to the natural rhythms of the world rather than upon the calculated needs of mankind. An economy based upon the needs of expenditure in today's world would be a contradiction in terms: it would negate itself at the moment it was put into practice, particularly given that the needs of expenditure cannot by definition be calculated. What was necessary was a completely new vision of the way society was structured so that the general economy could assume its appropriate form. In short, it required the reconstitution of heterogeneity.

Bataille tries to show that any form of restricted economy perverts the genuine aspirations of man because it treats productive needs as the primary, if not the only, needs that humanity has.

In point of fact, capitalism does not escape the logic of Bataille's dialectic: it does spend and it spends quite as uselessly, quite as prodigally as any other society. What is missing from capitalism is not the fact of expenditure but any sense of a joyous surpassing of limits. In so far as we spend, we do so grudgingly with an eye upon an ultimate accumulation. Expenditure, then, takes place in the spirit of universal meanness that Bataille identified with capitalism in such strong terms. Equally, this expenditure is not returned back to the community but is made to serve the aims of the market, which in the process is imbued with its own reality that exists independently of the real needs of mankind.

The ideological thrust of a restricted economy based on production has served to hide from us the fact that our natural propensity in itself creates a surplus of wealth. In so far as there is poverty in the world, it is not caused by a scarcity of economic means but by the fact that one person's surplus has been appropriated by another. Bataille expresses this as follows:

> It is assumed, today even more, that the world is poor and we must work. The world however is sick with wealth. A contrary sentiment maintains in place the inequality of conditions which cause us not to perceive what Peter lacks as being what is superfluous to Paul.[25]

Bataille's analysis of data is often flawed. But in many ways we might say that this is because he departs from his own postulates. By sometimes abstracting expenditure from its relation with accumulation, he does what he otherwise condemns: he turns it into a thing. In so doing he effectively turns his back on the concept of the general economy and establishes an inverted form of the restricted economy. This causes him to stop halfway in his analysis. He thus tends to make a fetish of expenditure. At times he even perceives this problem in terms of his own work:

> Writing this book in which I was saying that energy finally can only be wasted, I myself was using my energy, my time, working; my

research answered in a fundamental way the desire to add to the amount of wealth acquired for mankind. Should I say that under these conditions I sometimes could only respond to the truth of my book and could not go on writing it.[26]

Given the basis from which he started, it is of course hardly surprising that there should be inconsistencies in Bataille's work. This should not be treated as a reason for dismissing what he has to say. In many ways it should be considered if not as a virtue then as a mark of authenticity. Bataille never sought to establish a closed system. Quite the contrary, everything inclined him against such a possibility. He says himself that his work bears witness to what came up as the dice were thrown. As such it must be considered as a beginning not as an end.

Living as we do in an age dominated by the pure utilitarianism of a monetarist economics, which has made a cult of money to a degree that even Bataille would have found hard to believe, in which the necessity has been to allow the market to determine its own course independently of human needs, the vitality of his work becomes ever more apparent. At the beginning of this chapter, we noted how uncannily Bataille's thinking reads as a negation of monetarism. Now that the disastrous consequences of the monetarists' blinkered vision have become apparent to everyone, his work perhaps gains its most important application. This much is perhaps significant. Held up against the rationalist and humanist vision of Keynesian consensual economics, Bataille's contentions can appear inconsequential, but in its social ambition, Keynesian economics conceals the consequences of its economic determinism. The illusion of social welfarism is that of an evolutionary process towards a non-utilitarian based society. It implies a new Calvinism: by building now we would be able to enjoy the fruits of our labour later. Monetarism tore apart this social illusion. If it destroyed the modest gains of social welfarism, it also served to show us the lie on which its claims were based. Faced with the rapaciousness and sheer bankruptcy of an economy based on monetarist principles, Bataille's views no longer seem absurd.

Chapter 6

Death, communication and the experience of limits

As a sociologist, Bataille was determined to explore the very heart of things. He eschewed the analysis of the specialist who begins with the particular and builds up towards the general but rather sought first to establish a general framework within which to explore more particular data. He therefore put forward the idea of the general economy as a framework within which the study of social phenomena could be analysed.

Complementary to this and in many ways preceding it, however, he also sought to explore the inner aspects of being. This was not separable from the idea of the general economy, but provided the core of what Bataille believed was the most reliable and essential data, since it was only what lay within oneself and was directly experienced, that one could really speak about with a genuine claim to authority. For him the analysis of society, therefore, had to pass through an equally rigorous examination of the self.

Bataille also wanted to explore both the external and internal aspects of social being, since he considered that one without the other was incomplete. The idea of the general economy represents the external social element but while social relations are the fundamental element of human existence, it still makes no sense to analyse social relations independently of the inner subjectivity of the individuals comprised within a given social network. Bataille defined this individual exploration variously as 'inner experience' or 'the sovereign operation'. We will discuss this notion in detail later in this chapter. First, though, let us look at the existential frame of Bataille's conception of the individual being and the way the individual relates to society.

It will be recalled that Bataille values individualism and individual freedom but not in themselves, not as abstractions which serve to divorce the individual from social values. For Bataille it is impossible to conceive of individuals other than as social beings and thus as being separable from the society of which they are an integral part.

At the heart of the social lies the convergence of work and sexuality and this convergence is intimately linked to our understanding of death. Bataille dealt with this issue most fully in *Eroticism*, which was published in 1957 and in many ways provides the summation of his life's work.[1]

Bataille's reflections in *Eroticism* bring the central elements of his thought into relief and develop the argument put forward around the idea of the general economy. In the previous chapter we suggested that elements of Bataille's argument depart from the postulates of the general economy and in fact, as we will see, the ideas developed in *Eroticism* can serve to bring into question some of the contentions put forward in *The Accursed Share*. Some of the criticisms made of Bataille in the preceding chapter therefore arise from Bataille's own argument in *Eroticism*, and we can only conjecture how differently Bataille would have approached the idea of the general economy if he had been able to take into account his own anterior work.

The new data upon which Bataille most especially drew in establishing the basis of the argument in *Eroticism* comes from his study of prehistoric art, which arises out of his commission in 1953 to write a book about the cave art at Lascaux. This research resulted in a book published in 1955, together with several other articles dealing with the beginnings of humankind, and served to confirm Bataille's understanding of the relation of taboo and transgression, providing him with a wealth of information upon which to draw in exploring the basis of taboo. This especially gave him a fresh focus on the importance of work in man's social history.

For Bataille, human experience is an experience of limits and these limits are defined by the fact that the condition of life for human beings is the recognition of death.

Death is not essential for life. The most simple life forms, which reproduce by scissiparity, perhaps do not die but live in a sort of eternity. It may even be inaccurate to say that they reproduce, since everything leads us to believe that the being that separates in scissiparity simply replicates itself and the resultant creature remains identical with the being from which it has separated.

If death is not necessary to life at this basic level, it does seem that in order for life to develop it needs to negate itself: for life to become complex it seems to be necessary that it impose limits on itself; it needs, that is, death. At the same time and for the same reason, it needs sexual differentiation. For, in order to develop, life requires separation and then the mingling of that separation in an embrace of differentiation. Reciprocally, it needs my death, and through my death the continuity of the life process is affirmed. Therefore life emerges from death, which is its condition and foundation. Life creates death for its own purposes. But at the same time life also remains the negation of death. It fears, condemns and tries to shut out what it nevertheless cannot do without; it correlatively needs sexual differentiation and the separation of being. Death and reproduction therefore negate and affirm the process of life. And, to emphasise the extent of this dependency, birth and death meet in the sexual act.

On this basis, Bataille asserts that eroticism affirms life to the point of death. Not only that, it also affirms life even in death. Both death and sex bring with them a residue, experienced even at a primitive level, for the loss of the continuity of being that had been the condition of scissiparity. This residue is anguish, for life asserts itself at the expense of the living being, which is caught in a double bind, desiring simultaneously to return to the comfort and undifferentiation of continuous being (when nothing existed that was other to it), while at the same time wishing to surpass its limits and unite with the otherness it fears even as it desires it, seeking to transcend the separation that exists between itself and the other. The motivation for such desire is that it will in the process overcome death and return to continuity in a higher form. Through differentiation, life, therefore, creates our sense of otherness and instills within us a sense of separation from our own sources. As a sentient being, then, I can never know another being's experience of life no matter how much it may remain analogous to my own. An unbridgeable gap exists between us which no desire can ever completely transcend. As Bataille puts it, 'Our existence is an exasperated attempt to complete being.'[2]

Anguish is therefore present in all sexualized living beings. But for most of life, for vegetation and animals it remains contained within a very limited frame. Plants rise upwards and wilt if they are deprived of the nourishment which sustains them. Animals become more clearly aware of the separation of their beings, but only at set periods: when they mate they do so in response to an exigency that tears at them and serves not their own personal regeneration but that of the species. They have no consciousness of themselves as separate beings, their only 'consciousness' (if this is the right word) is of their species-being. In so far as they are aware of the separation of being it is expressed only through the anguish of the species.

Only for mankind is the anguish of being embedded in the individual, because only humans are aware of death. At least, if animals are aware of death it is only to a limited extent. They may fear death, but in so far as they act to preserve life, against a predator or against the process of life itself, they do so only in response to the imperative needs of immediacy. They do not respond to death itself. They neither welcome it nor seek to flee it; their only concern is a primeval sense of the need for the preservation of life.

The increase of anguish the awareness of death brings to human beings is incommensurate with anything else in the animal kingdom. With awareness comes the will to flee, to postpone, or even to outwit death. Humans clothe themselves, build houses and vainly seek to give themselves the security that will re-assert continuity within the frame of their own lives. They do so vainly because death will always be there, lying in wait and ready to seize them at the most opportune, or inopportune, moment. Humans know this full well, but nevertheless their urge to preserve becomes primal. And yet at the same time we contain death within us and can at times welcome its embrace.

The paradox that Bataille sees as being the condition of life is here clearly revealed. For mankind's desires in this respect are paradoxical to an extreme degree. On the one hand we wish to live and we fear death to the extent that we seek with every fibre of our being to preserve our lives and elude the clutch of death. And yet at the same time, life itself – abstracted from the context in which we live – horrifies us even more and there are circumstances in which we come to desire its annulment and welcome death. For life to continue beyond a certain point or in circumstances we consider intolerable is felt by us to be worse than death. Therein lies the basis of the death instinct that Freud elucidated. Death has its attractions as well as its terrors, and this is where it is connected with sex: 'in sexual anguish there is a sadness of death, an apprehension of death which is rather vague but which we will never be able to shake off.'[3] At the same time, myths, like those of the Wandering Jew or those connected with vampirism, make it plain that if there is one thing we fear more than death it is not dying, or not being able to die. That this is also something unique to us is emphasised by the fact that in nature, suicide is unique to the human species.

Despite this urge to build and to deny the inevitability of death, humans nevertheless pay homage to the ultimate triumph of death and even celebrate it through the festival and through rituals that have the double purpose of binding the community together and recognising the precariousness of the conditions of life. Death is from this perspective the affirmation of life as well as its negation; its consecration as well as its ruin.

For Bataille, then, the recognition of death in the human sphere results in the sentiment of eroticism, which contains within it a simultaneous affirmation of life combined with the recognition of death. Let us emphasise the point by giving Bataille's definition, which was referred to earlier: 'eroticism is the assenting to life up to the point of death; . . . eroticism is the assenting to life even in death.'[4] At the same time, the sensibility to which eroticism responds is one that undercuts our own sense of being. It thus 'calls the inner life into play. In human consciousness, eroticism is within man's consciousness what calls his being in question.'[5] As such eroticism is central to the human condition, it is in eroticism that our specificity as humans is asserted and through eroticism that we are marked psychologically as being different from other animals.

Within animals, sexual activity responds only to a mechanical necessity. It implies no *inner* need. The inner need that has developed within humans (or perhaps it was their condition, a necessary pre-requisite without which they could not have become human) has arisen through a play between contradictory impulses. In becoming aware of the reality of death, humans sought to flee it, to provide themselves with a security that would deny the very awareness they found difficult to accept. To achieve this sense of security required work. And work in its turn needed to be protected from disorder (the disorder of violence and exuberance). That is, it became a psychological necessity to rationalise work. This involved a collective crime that founded a notion of guilt that took effect in the human mind in an analogous way to the primal scene which we saw discussed in the previous chapter. To this end prohibitions took form within mankind's consciousness: taboos therefore came to be erected as an essential protection for the structure of society, and thereby became internally necessary for mankind's species-being, since the perceived need was transferred from the social into man's psychological being. It is on this specific point that Bataille's argument becomes more complex than that of Norman O. Brown. While he might agree that the taboo would take shape as an infantile fantasy in each generation, this does not mean that it is purely to be ascribed to a neurotic basis.

Bataille would doubtless agree with Freud that the primal scene took shape as an actual event (although not necessarily as a specific occurrence that can be conceptualised in the way Freud did), that stands at the heart of human psychological reality. He would certainly not agree with Brown that it can be conjured away by being recognised: if we are to come to terms with it, then it must be by confronting its reality, which lies in mankind's effort to found its essence in opposition to nature. For Bataille it is the very prodigality of life, transferred into the human soul, that makes taboos a necessity, since, 'unchecked [life] annihilates what it has created'.[6] What is essential to realise about the taboo is that it can never be externally imposed: it always takes form in response to an inner imperative.

The imposition of the taboo implied at the same time the need to transgress it, the provision for which primitive society made within a ritual form that allowed, at specific times and occasions, free play and which gave shape to the myths that provided the basis for human society. This was the time that the world would be 'turned upside down' and all that had been denied in the cause of the principle of work was brought back into the social sphere. Transgression was thus an essential component of the taboo. It did not stand outside it, nor was the impulse behind transgression to subvert the taboo but on the contrary to ensure its effectiveness. Transgression, therefore, 'does not deny the taboo, but transcends and completes it'.[7]

Transgression was a dynamic element of society that served to prevent stagnation whilst at the same time maintaining stability. It was not a question of a need to transgress specific taboos – there was no correspondence in this sense between a taboo and the transgressive impulse. The two spheres were in fact necessarily incommensurate. The structure of transgression directly served to give expression to the idea of the taboo in its generality. It was in this sense that transgression never served to undermine the specificity of taboos. Transgression should equally not be confused with a sense of disorder: it obeyed its own rules (which were often more rigorous than those of the taboo) and implied the consciousness, never the absence, of limits.

The interplay between taboo and transgression served as the basis for a social structure whose foundation lay in individual consciousness, so that the same pattern was repeated both within the individual and within the society. Where, in the social sphere, transgression was most immediately present within the festival, in the personal sphere its domain was that of eroticism. From this perspective, 'the inner experience of eroticism demands from the person involved an equal sensitivity towards the anguish which provides the basis for interdiction and the desire which tends to violate it.' At the same time, 'the objective fact of reproduction calls into question within the inner consciousness the feeling of self, the feeling of being and of the limits of the isolate being.'

At the same time, and complementary to the play between taboo and transgression, there is a subsidiary play between the life instinct and the impulse for death, which Bataille characterised as a conflict between continuity and discontinuity. Life, in its unfolding, likes to consider itself as a continuous process: as living beings we would like to be able to live as though we were not going to die. Death breaks this continuity, rudely inserting discontinuity into the structure of the universe. However, as it does so, death asserts at the same time the greater continuity of existence, a continuity from which we have been plucked by being born and thrown into the world of differentiation that is maintained by life. Through death our separation from others and from the universe is broken and we are restored to a sense of primary harmony. Without death we would exist as separate beings ignorant of and irrevocably separated from anything that exists outside ourselves. Death, then, is violence, but it is at the same time communication. It is the consciousness of death, not life, that makes community a possibility. Death (or rather the consciousness we have of it) therefore lies at the heart of being, without which we would not be what we are.

In its transgressive role, sexuality brings together both the awareness of death and the need for work, since it represents both a challenge to the principle of work and a recognition of death. Our sensibility is tied to a lost continuity framed by our awareness of death. As they exist in themselves, animals are entire to themselves; not knowing that they will die, their life is for them a continuous process. This luxury is denied to human beings since death is the recognition of the discontinuity of life and so, by destroying the discontinuous being, death affirms the underlying continuity of being. In sexual activity the assertion of the life process and its concomitant need to build, to accumulate its resources, is maintained by reproduction, but the sexual act contains within it at the same time a total effusion of pleasure that simultaneously denies this utilitarian function. Sexual activity at once affirms and denies the principle of work, just as, from the opposite angle, it both affirms and denies the pleasure principle. Bataille therefore asserts that there is an indelible connection between what he calls 'the promise of life implicit in eroticism and the sensuous aspect of death'.[8]

Eroticism is life momentarily overflowing its limits, life in its richest, most abundant possibilities. But these possibilities are framed by the realisation of death. If the sexual act is life at its most abundant, it is also – so to speak – the denial, or the refutation, of life, for it opens the door to death and it lies on the threshold that reveals death before us. Within it there is, therefore, the recognition of our own mortality and the discontinuity of our being. At the same time it is also the mark of our intimate relation with nature. In eroticism we merge back into nature as our body dissolves into that of the beloved. In this carnality, paradise is momentarily recovered and we merge into our surroundings as we interpenetrate with each other's bodies and so any distinction between nature and culture vanishes.

The denial of eroticism – which is particularly strong within our culture – is at the same time an attempt to deny and close out death and our connection with nature. It is a characteristic of a homogeneous society that refuses to recognise the element of disorder implied by eroticism. It is generally denied in two complementary ways: through restricting sexual activity to its reproductive function and upholding an ideal of chastity or through a legitimation of indulgence in animal sexuality, that is by sanctioning libertinism and sexual promiscuity. For Bataille, libertinism was as much an emanation of the urge for the denial of eroticism as was puritan detachment. As he states: 'Eroticism only cedes sovereignty by degrading itself to animal activity.'[9] But even denied, eroticism still defines our species-being; it remains what separates us from beasts. But it does so only in conjunction with its opposite, which is work.

Since social life needs to be regulated through the interplay of profane and sacred, so personal life too needs to be aware of the relation between taboo and transgression. The denial of this necessity, whether by puritanism or by libertinism, is analogous with the denial of the sacred and has the same roots. Let us, then, take a closer look at the denial both of the erotic and the energy of the transgressive, the key to which, Bataille, believed lies within the ideology of Christianity.

We have already seen how strongly Bataille felt that Christian ideology had been instrumental in giving legitimation to the introduction of the work ethic to all areas of social life, in the process serving to cut it adrift from transgression. The havoc that it played in personal relations in the realm of sexuality was no less deleterious (it was of course part of the same process), for it has served to tear our inner experience from itself.

The ideological truth of the Judeo/Christian tradition is based upon a clash of interests that undermines the urge towards equilibrium and harmony which most non-Christian societies have seen as being the essential aspiration of social and personal being. This is something that has many implications, but fundamentally the creation of a transcendental, dualistic tradition, which has reached its fullest form in the Judeo-Christian-Islam conjunction, meant the separation of the world into hostile interest groups that would compete with each other. This was the definition of Christianity that Bataille gave: 'It is the negation of human sovereignty to benefit a transcendent sovereignty founded on personal superiority. God invites us to humility and death in order to share sovereignty.'[10]

Everything leads us to believe that human thought is essentially dualistic, in so far as thought generally bases itself on a separation of distinct opposing elements. The yin/yang principle of Chinese thought is a particularly complex example. But the Christian tradition introduced into this fundamental dualist pattern both a moral value and a transcendence by which opposing elements were no longer complementary to each other but came to engage in mortal conflict. This conflict was revealed in its purest form in Zoroastrianism, where good and evil were both conceived in an absolute sense and – though the conflict between them was deadly – they could not contaminate each other. The Christian tradition tempered this purity by introducing the notion of sin into the conflict. Where Zoroastrianism exists before the fall so that, if life is evil, it is so absolutely and there can be no possibility of salvation, Christianity posits the fall at the essence of our being: we exist with the reality of having committed a sin from which we can be delivered only by means of penitence; our salvation is even then reserved for an afterlife which will judge the extent of our repentance. Bataille explains that 'man of the dualistic conception is opposite to archaic man in that there is no longer any intimacy between him and this world. This world is in fact immanent to him but is so in so far as he is no longer characterised by intimacy, in so far as he is defined by things, and is himself a thing, being a distinctly separated being.'[11] Christianity is thus a condition of servitude. With it begins the possibility of class society and the alienation of the individual from society.

While the association of Christianity with sin and guilt is widely accepted, Bataille introduces another complicating and paradoxical element. For if it was Christianity that introduced the idea of original sin, we can also see in Christianity a will to deny the reality of sin (as it is tied to the transgression) and the sense of collective guilt with which it is associated. The urge of Christianity is towards a guilt-free condition. 'There is within Christianity a will not to be guilty,' he writes.

It is precisely this will to escape from guilt that is the sickness brought to the world by Christianity.

We have seen how important Bataille considered the idea of collective guilt and how it provided the foundation for the social world that defined mankind. The sense of guilt was the essential element of our being, but it was guilt without an object. Here Bataille's interest in gnostic and Manichean thought becomes manifest: guilt was inherent in the condition of being alive: we are only guilty through having allowed ourselves to be born and so torn from universal continuity. The guilt has nothing to do with our own personal being, but inheres to us *because we are human beings*. There can therefore be no possible escape from it and no possibility of salvation.

Christianity overturns this elemental sense of guilt by transforming it into a fault that inheres in mankind. It needs to give it an object and thus the notion of original sin arises. The importance of introducing such an object is that it brings into existence the possibility of salvation: if we are shown to be at fault, then we can rectify our crime and regain our primal innocence. We achieve this only through strict adherence with the taboo, which in the process is legitimated against transgressive behaviour (rather than being complementary to it). Instead of guilt, it is now the abstract conception of the law that becomes the fundamental condition of human society and transgression, the witness of man's guilt, is expelled. Everything is directed towards the end of satisfying an object (i.e. God) which the Christian spirit sees mankind as having offended. The need is no longer to frame work through an interplay between taboo and transgression, but rather to drive out the trans-gression, which represents our fall, and so create the condition whereby we can be saved. This requires our own effort to become responsible and so wash away our fault. Work is in the process sanctified as the only good, against which all other activity is measured. And in as much as we obey the law (which is work and is also God), we can learn not to be guilty.

From this perspective, Bataille considered Christianity to be essentially anti-religious, to even represent an assault on the very principle of religion, based as it is in communication and the sacred. To appreciate what this involves we need to be clear about terminology, because Bataille is using terms in a way that often goes against customary use.

By religion Bataille does not in any sense refer to belief in a god. Equally he does not mean what Marx meant when he defined religion in the famous passage from the *Critique of Hegel's Philosophy of Right* as an 'inverted consciousness of the world'. Quite the contrary, for Bataille 'religion' referred to mankind's inner truth, which Christianity has always sought to deny if not destroy.

This sense of religion is tied up with Bataille's notion of society and with the sacred. We have seen how Bataille equated the 'sacred' with 'communication'. The religious sentiment, therefore, is born of man's need for communication. In denying this need for communication, Christianity denies religion, which is an immanent element of our being, the element that stands for our attempt to heal the rupture between ourselves and our experience of life. It is what cements our social relations and makes possible a relative social harmony.

For Bataille, Christianity broke this relative harmony and was anti-religious in the sense that it abrogated the sacred, denying mankind in favour of a transcendent deity to whom mankind owed obeisance. The impulse of Christianity has always been to destroy social bonds by asserting that the only genuine bond is between man and the god who is presented as his creator. We no longer define ourselves in relation to our reality within the world but through our relation with something that is beyond the world. This further reinforces the extent to which the taboo is affirmed at the expense of transgression. In this way the taboo ceases to be a purely temporal boundary necessary for social bonding, but becomes established as an absolute principle (God, law and work, the principle of good). The same thing is true of the transgression, which can no longer be recognised as inherent to, and a temporal creation of, the taboo, but becomes something to be definitively expelled. Its principle is no less absolute: it becomes the Devil, crime and euphoria, the principle of evil. The transgressive principle, as it relates to effusion, is expelled from this life to an afterworld conceptualised as the Christian heaven, and to which we can gain access only by means of complete compliance with the taboo.

As pure effusion sexuality personifies the principle of transgression (by being what is opposed to work). It therefore becomes problematic for Christianity to the extent that it affirms transgression rather than the reproduction of the species. A need to deny its transgressive force therefore becomes manifest. However, it cannot expel sexual activity as such without nullifying the very basis of the regeneration of the species. The need, therefore, is to refuse the transgressive aspects of sexuality while retaining those that relate to reproduction and healthy relations between the sexes (as the foundation for a 'natural' sexuality that can as much be found in pure libertinism as in sex aimed at propagation). In either case, sex is no longer a laceration, a tearing apart of our being that calls our sense of what we are into question, but becomes domesticated as a utilitarian value in whose name eroticism itself is denied. Non-utilitarian sexuality becomes a malediction and is denounced as 'perverse'.[12]

For Christianity, the problem remains of how to affirm the reproductive act without recognising the malediction that effusive sexuality brings with it. Because what is necessary above all for Christianity is to diffuse the 'dangerous' quality of eroticism, a danger that lies not primarily in the fact that it is an expression of pleasure, but in the recognition of the discontinuity within the life process, of which it offers a glimpse through the fact that it contains both life and death within itself and provides their point of intersection. As such it simultaneously enriches our sense of both the anguish of being as well as its plenitude.

Furthermore, if Christianity expelled the expectation contained in transgressive behaviour to a transcendent afterlife, then it follows that there has to be a continuum from life itself to such an afterlife. This requires a denial of death, at least of that death that implies discontinuity and rupture. Christianity could not deny death itself, which has an objective quality. But it could deny the causative link between birth and death which is represented in the sex act itself, containing as it does the anguish of both the promise of life and the inevitable surge towards death. A preliminary rupture with death is thereby established. But the problem remains that it is not possible to reject sexuality entirely without at the same time denying birth, something which would imply also a denial of life itself. Sexuality must therefore be purified and abstracted from the contagion of death to be affirmed purely and simply as the principle of life. This does not simply reduce sexuality to its reproductive qualities: it affirms it as a utilitarian principle that reduces the life experience itself to the state of being an object. Life now becomes fully equated with work. Rather than being formed as a psychological reality necessary to an existence that needed to be protected from the consequences of its own disorder, now the taboo becomes the principle of man's whole *raison d'être*. Bataille thus defined the Christian God as representing nothing but a 'hypostasis of work'.

But Bataille notes that 'Christianity could not get rid of impurity altogether'[13]: it was forced to admit transgression within the bounds of a 'necessary evil'. Such an admission must serve to nullify any efficacy embodied in transgression, which, to have meaning, can exist only relational to the original taboo.

The logic of the dialectic requires that whatever is thrown out through the door enters by the window. In so far as the principle of Christianity works on the principle that the taboo must be sustained without admitting the legitimacy of its transgression, then the transgression, if it cannot be destroyed, still needs to be neutralised. The corollary of reducing it to its functional aspect, is that it leads also to the exaltation of libidinal pleasure divorced from any psychic involvement. There therefore arises, complementary to the puritan impulse, the need to profane the world and make all activity conform to functional needs. Non-reproductive sexuality can still be affirmed, but only if it denies its basis in transgression and the sacred. Libertinism becomes a complement to puritanism, providing an equally utilitarian basis to obscure transgression as it treats the object of desire as pure possession rather than as a possibility of communication. In such a world, eroticism starts to disappear. Bataille therefore asserts that 'in an entirely profane world nothing would be left but animal mechanism'.[14]

The recovery of eroticism and what it means to our existence thus becomes a fundamental task of atheism. Bataille defined three forms of eroticism. These were 1) the *eroticism of bodies*, in which a violation of the sense of individual being is experienced (this is, in fact, the inner experience of sacrifice, when one feels oneself being devoured by one's partner, but in which one remains acutely aware of discontinuous existence); 2) the *eroticism of hearts*, in which the lover perceives the beloved in totality. This prolongs the eroticism of bodies to the point that a momentary recovery of continuum is experienced, deepened by the fusion of bodies: the couple become a joint egoism, but this imposes a new discontinuum and it offers only an image of the miracle of a desirable continuity of being; 3) *spiritual eroticism*, in which we no longer depend on a partner to open out on to continuity; in this state death becomes unable to extinguish being, and eroticism is affirmed in the full approbation of life.[15]

Eroticism serves the purposes of love; it is an explosion, a bursting of life, and it needs to be returned to its rightful place, which lies at the heart of the sacred. It represents both a mediation point between ourselves and the forces of nature and at the same time both differentiates as well as emphasising our essential unity. The sex act must, indeed, be equated with sacrifice: 'The lover strips bare the beloved of her identity no less that the blood-stained priest his human or animal victim. The woman in the hands of her assailant is despoiled of her being.'[16] Against the Christian urge to reduce sexuality, there arises the need to affirm it in its pure effusiveness and with its relation with death accepted unreservedly and joyfully. Again the relation with sacrifice is made explicit: 'It is the common business of sacrifice to bring life and death into harmony, to give death the upsurge of life, life the momentousness and the vertigo of death opening onto the unknown".[17] The implications this raises was what Bataille sought to follow through with his idea of 'inner experience'.

Of all the influences on Bataille we discussed in Chapter 1 we did not mention the person who perhaps had the most decisive and lasting influence of all on him. This was Colette Peignot, with whom he lived from 1934 to 1938. In order to fully understand Bataille's idea of 'inner experience', it is essential for us to consider the influence of Colette Peignot, who also adopted the name Laure.

Colette was from a wealthy Parisian bourgeois background and gravitated to the surrealist and communist circles during the twenties. She had lived with Jean Bernier, an important figure in *Clarté*, the communist group that had collaborated with the Surrealist Group in 1926. After she split up with Bernier she had lived in Berlin and then, to experience the Russian Revolution, had lived among a family of kulaks before falling so seriously ill that her brother had to travel to the USSR to bring her back to France.

Back in Paris, she lived with Boris Souvarine, one of the founders of the French Communist Party, but also one of the first to perceive the dangers of Stalinism, who had left the Party as early as 1923 to found an oppositional communist group. Colette was actively involved in the organisation of Souvarine's Cercle Communiste Démocratique, in which Bataille participated, and was mainly responsible for financing the circle's journal, *La Critique sociale*,[18] and published several articles in it, mostly connected with the Russian Revolution, under the pseudonym 'Claude Araxe'[19]

Bataille had known Colette for some years before they became emotionally involved in 1934 in the wake of the break-up of Bataille's first marriage.[20] They had an extremely intense, violent and rending relationship which Bataille compared with that of Cathy and Heathcliff in *Wuthering Heights*. When she died in 1938, Bataille was overcome with a profound sense of guilt and sorrow that marked him for many years and from which he perhaps never entirely recovered. As in Emily Brontë's tale, Bataille remained haunted by the spectre of Colette for a long time after she died.[21] The whole of *La Somme Athéologique* was really addressed to her and can be considered as a working through of his relationship with her. Indeed, everything Bataille wrote during the decade that followed her death can be seen as a sort of communication with her beyond the grave. More immediately, though there can be little doubt that it was because of Laure that Bataille fully recognised all the implications raised by considering the nature of the sacred in contemporary life.

Laure had reflected on the sacred through a series of luminous texts, the central one of which was written as a response to Michel Leiris's 'The Sacred in Everyday Life'.[22] For Laure the sacred was an 'infinitely rare state of grace'. It was realised at any moment when one feels one's own individuality slip away to become realised within universal movement. As such it was the moment of communication *par excellence* that could be located within one's own being only by taking one's sensibility to the depths. It was only when one had stripped oneself bare that one could discover the point at which self and other become one and a universal communion is perceived: my desires become at one with those of all people. Thus, the sacred was the 'infinitely rare moment in which the "eternal wealth" that each person carries within the self enters into life to find itself carried along, *realised*, in universal movement.'[23]

It seems that it was Laure who had encouraged Bataille to establish Acéphale as a framework to follow through ideas of the sacred in contemporary life. Acéphale was thus to be a sort of place of communication at which the movement of individual desires would gain its own momentum to become carried into a collective consecration.

Central to Laure's writing is the problem of communication, something very much central to surrealist concerns, and her starting point certainly begins in surrealism which, according to Bataille, 'seduced' her. Surrealism had set itself the problem of human expression in all its forms, and this implied a release from the social obligation to communicate. For the surrealists, that is, there was no necessity to obey the utilitarian needs of social language, which was something that distorted the real needs of communication. This created a dilemma for all surrealists and was something that Bataille felt most acutely: How, if I reject the utilitarian function of literature, can I use language to communicate, since does the process of writing down or publishing a work imply in itself a compromise with the very utility one hoped to deny?

Laure solved this problem in a very direct way: she never published anything in her lifetime, and she did not even show anything she had written to Bataille, for he confessed himself 'astonished' when he read through her papers after her death. She was obsessed with a double trauma of separation, the first represented by death, the second by the fact of sharing one's life with others. Both were essential to life, the only thing that was worthwhile in life, and yet both brought an overwhelming sense of anguish and loss. 'It's simple,' she writes in one of her poems, 'the impossibility of true exchange.' Yet this did not satisfy her since she also wrote, 'I need the public.' This discordance is one that can never be resolved except provisionally and the step necessary to make such accommodation is one in which Laure was not prepared to indulge. Bataille was later to write that 'communication' only takes place *between two people who risk themselves.*[24] And in a sense it was as a continuation of the risk involved in his relationship with Laure that Bataille thereafter contemplated his relationship with his work.

We can also see that the central themes of his later work are already announced by Laure's writing. She defined the idea of the sovereign operation exactly in terms that Bataille would later take up: 'Poetic work is sacred when it is the creation of a topical event, communication felt as *a denuding*. It is violated of itself, denudation, communication to others of the reason for living, in which this very reason for living is itself displaced.'[25] There seems to be little doubt that the motivation of Colette's life was towards transformation in the alchemical sense, a quest to discover the gold of existence. Her assumed name (Laure = l'or) itself represents a process of transmutation. And it is for this reason that the demand to communicate reasons for living must, at the same moment, itself be displaced, for it is always to be a question of opening up possibilities, accepting the dynamism of the universe and refusing to privilege reasons for living in isolation from the life process. This is what she means by speaking of a 'topical event', topical referring not to an isolated, ephemeral occurrence, but to what is relevant at the particular time at which one is writing.

Bataille often seems a little in awe of Colette: 'No one,' he wrote, 'has ever seemed as uncompromising and pure as she was, nor more "sovereign"'[26] Certainly it was her example, and her uncompromising determination to face the consequences of living at the extremes of experience that Bataille resolved to engage with in exploring the idea of inner experience.

Although Bataille often uses the terminology and context of the expression of Christian mysticism when he discusses his inner experience, he is nevertheless careful – even if he perceived analogies between his own experience and that of mystics like Saint Teresa – to dissociate himself from the objective experience of Christian mysticism. This procedure, which Bataille identified as 'inner experience' or 'the sovereign operation', appears to lie less within the frame of mysticism than with that of shamanism.

One is a little reluctant to invoke shamanism in such a context since it has been devalued by the impulse of recent pseudo-anthropological works like those of Castaneda, which assimilate shamanism to Western discourse in a completely saccharine way, that is, as a path to self-knowledge, and self-improvement, something which has nothing to do with the experience of shamanism (which is thereby reduced to a means of utilitarianism).

While Bataille's experience is entirely framed by Western concepts and he does retain some of the terminology of Christian mysticism, nevertheless there can be no doubt that the experience he conveys has nothing to do with union with a transcendent God. As far as 'God' is invoked in Bataille's writings it is as something unknown, ineffable and, in fact, unknowable. As such it certainly goes beyond anything that is proper to Western mysticism.

For Bataille, inner experience had to be a plunge into the heart of being. The mystics sometimes approached such a state, but they did so only by default, as a by-product, so to speak, of their attempted communication with a transcendent God. As Bataille distinguished the content of inner experience from mysticism, he also distinguished it from Eastern disciplines like Tantrism which he considered to involve a renunciation of being. Such a renunciation seeks ultimately to master existence, something Bataille believed to be against the essential movement of inner experience which had to be confronted on its own terms, not on the conditions laid down beforehand by the subject seeking to engage it. Any attempt at control or mastery would serve to devalue the experience. Although meditation was a means to approach it, the essential was that one had to be chosen by the inner experience itself and not impose oneself into it. Any attempt to induce the experience was similarly doomed to failure and condemned by Bataille, who despised the use of artificial stimulants or drugs. One must not go looking for inner experience: it had to come and find you. In *Inner Experience* he describes his feeling as he sensed himself becoming a tree: 'I feel myself, in the darkness of my room, becoming a tree and even a tree struck by lightning.'[27] But he felt that he could only experience this by accident; it could not be something that could be experienced through desire. It responds to his sense of the immanence of knowledge, which he expressed in this way: 'Immanence is received and is not the result of searching for it; it is wholly and entirely governed by chance.'[28] For all of these reasons it does seem that the analogies of Bataille's experience with that of shamanism are not at all inappropriate. Although, according to Roger Caillois, at the time of the College of

Sociology, Bataille had seriously aspired to become a shaman, Bataille himself does not appear to have made the comparison in relation to inner experience. Nevertheless there do seem strong reasons for exploring Bataille's experience in relation to that of the shaman.

In both *Inner Experience* and *Guilty* there are numerous references to events that read like incidents from a shamanic journey. This one from *Guilty* can be cited in particular:

> The way goes through a haunted region, which is, however, haunted (with ghosts of delight and fear). Beyond: are a blind man's motions, eyes wide open, arms stretching out, staring at the sun, and inside he's turning to light. Imagine now that a change takes place. There's a bursting into flame that's so sudden the idea of substance seems empty; place, exteriority, and image become so many empty words, and the words that have least shifted, *fusion* and *light* – are by nature incomprehensible.'[29]

Like the shaman's journey, Bataille's inner experience begins in sickness and a crisis of life. As a sickness it is one that is as much of the mind as the body. Although Bataille was physically ill when he began to explore the idea of inner experience (a sickness that led, in 1942, to his leaving the Bibliothèque Nationale), it was also his sense of loss over the death of Laure that motivated the plunge into himself that is documented through inner experience. The essence of the experience of shamanism lies in the wound, in the terrible wound that opens up being. One could only become a shaman through being sick and following the path of the sickness to its limit, to its substantiality, which is death. To become a shaman one had to cure oneself by a confrontation with death.

One does get a real sense that this is what Bataille faced. In the various parts of *La Somme athéologique*, and also in the strange hybrid text *The Impossible*, there is an overriding feel of a journey into the very heart of being, in which Bataille risks becoming overwhelmed by the dark forces of life and that he does almost die in the process, before returning back into society in a way reintegrated with life.

Bataille's sense of inner experience raises his objective relation to Christianity, something which is complex, and I think we would be making an error if we were to situate him within a tradition of anti-clericalism. His position also appears to be rather singular among the surrealists, most of whom rejected Christianity in a rather guttural and unreflexive way, that is, they viewed Christianity purely as a symbol for repressive and authoritarian values and it was, as such, to be rejected as a whole. 'Everything that is collapsing, shifty, infamous, sullying and grotesque is summed up for me in this single word: God', wrote André Breton. Very few surrealists saw any need to take Christianity seriously in its ideas. For most of them their rejection of it was definitive and implied no sense of nostalgia. Nietzsche's announcement of the death of God meant little to them in specific terms: since God had never been alive there was little point in concerning oneself about his death.[30] For Breton or Péret the absence of God was not at all a problem in the way it was for Bataille. The latter's exploration of what the lack of God in contemporary life meant was therefore certainly much more profound. His relation to the idea of God is expressed in these lines: 'The big lie: existing in this world under these conditions and thinking up a God who's like us! A God who calls himself *me*!'[31]

On the other hand, unlike most French surrealists, Bataille did not feel scarred by a Christian upbringing. Quite the contrary, it was the lack of religion in his childhood that he seems to have felt most acutely, and his adolescent rebellion was directed against his parents' lack of faith: he converted to Catholicism, made every effort to live a life in accord with Christian precepts, and was even drawn towards the idea of becoming a priest.

Even though he came to violently reject Christianity, his experience of it does not seem to have left any psychological scars. He did not rebel against Christian repression. Although he tells us that he rejected Christianity because it had caused pain to the woman he loved, one does not get the impression that he had renounced Christianity because he felt it to be oppressive. It was rather a sense of disappointment: Christianity was unable to satisfy his need for the absolute. His turning against it was similar to his turning away from his parents, and he seems to have felt that it had betrayed him in a similar way, since it was unable to give him a framework to come to terms with the intensity of his religious feelings. Christianity was too complacent. It was, in fact, not religious enough. It represented a poverty of existence not, as a religion should, its abundance. 'Christianity's impoverishment,' he wrote, 'lies in its will (through asceticism) to escape a state in which fragility or non-substance is painful.'[32] He returns to this frequently in his writings; it should not be a matter of turning one's back on Christianity, but rather of going beyond it, creating what he called a 'hyper-Christianity' which would give meaning to the experience of life as it was really lived. It was this that Bataille described as an 'atheology'.

It is here that Nietzsche's experience was so decisive for him. Nietzsche's proclamation of the 'death of God' struck a chord in Bataille.

God is dead, of course, of having been exposed as nothing but a projection of mankind. While it is therefore necessary to rebuild a new sense of the sacred that Christianity had destroyed, there was also a need to work with Christian concepts rather than simply dismiss them. For Bataille, to do the latter would be to make the same error that Christianity itself made.

If we can say that Bataille's encounter with his being in inner experience was comparable to that of the shaman's journey, there nevertheless remains a vital element that is lacking from it, which is the social element. The shaman experiences the world not simply for himself but on behalf of the community. Bataille's experience on the other hand remained, no matter what he might have liked, an individual encounter which had little collective resonance. It was an act of heterogeneity in a society that had not so much outlawed heterogeneous activity as refused to recognise it. At least it can recognise it only in so far as it can transform it into something homogeneous, that is to the extent that it can reduce it to the level of a thing. It is this that can serve to legitimate an experience such as Bataille's which would otherwise be considered aberrant: it serves the purposes of self-knowledge.

Bataille of course refused such an alibi and tried to undermine it with the introduction of the idea of non-knowledge, but this was not enough to give any collective dimension to his own work. Before engaging in inner experience, though, he had believed in the possibility of recovering a collective sense of the sacred and this was the basis for the activities of Acéphale.

We shall no doubt never know whether Bataille really intended to perform the human sacrifice he proposed. All of our information about this incident is charged with ambivalence and clearly responded to Bataille's taste for provocation. Certainly, though, he wanted to consecrate the activity of Acéphale by means of an extreme act that would give form to the intimacy that bound together those who participated within the group.

There was an immediate paradox in the structure of Acéphale, since, despite the will to be 'headless', everyone was well aware that it was Bataille who was the motivating force behind it and without him the group would not have existed. It seems that there was a certain play on this apparent contradiction. Georges Duthuit mentions referring to Bataille as the 'head of the acephali'[33], while Jules Monnerot has spoken about the quality of 'heresiarch' that Bataille assumed.

This is something inherent in any form of collective activity in the contemporary world – is it possible for it to form in an organised way? Is it not inevitable that it must rely on individual initiative to initiate and sustain it? This difficulty is even more acute when it comes to trying to re-enact the public mechanism that once pertained in respect of a sacred act like that of ritual sacrifice.

Is it not clear that the experience of sacrifice must be impossible in contemporary society, since everything we know about sacrificial practices suggests that it was entirely free from any sense of individual guilt – the guilt of which it was the expression was undoubtedly collective? Sacrifice cannot be experienced in individual terms, and so it would seem to follow that the frame established by Western individualism would make the experience an essentially alien one for us. How can we recover the social frame that has been lost? Bataille realised that this was a problem and knew that such an experience needed to be framed by a collective movement founded in a complicity he hoped would be enough to re-establish a genuine social bonding. But how could this be shaped? Has not any sense of collective guilt been definitively displaced onto the individual, and as such irrevocably divorced from any real relation with society? How can one recover a sense of collective guilt unless one addresses the question consciously, something that would necessarily vitiate the possibility of that guilt really being felt in a genuinely collective way?

Equally, it would appear that to wish to partake of the experience of the sacred must be vain since that there is not *one* experience of sacrifice. Neither ethnology nor psychology has penetrated any essence that can serve in any way to define the universal experience of sacrifice. Since sacrifice does seem to be universal, it would seem to follow that there must be such an essence, but its roots are buried deep and overlaid by the actual practice over millennia, which has served to imbue the act with local concerns that depend on the particular social circumstances in which they are to be found.

For this reason it does not seem likely that there is an actual inner experience of sacrifice and therefore Bataille's will to reach the core of the experience of sacrifice seems a vain one. The one thing we can assert about the essence of sacrifice is that it is expression of a collective sense of guilt, but this is to say no more than that it has an elemental importance for mankind. The sacrificial experience – at least in its collective form[34] – appears inseparable from its form and can only be experienced within the social context in which it takes place. It needed complicity, 'first in the crime itself, and then in ignoring it, [that] unites humanity in the most intimate way possible.'[35] Yet has not any such sense of complicity been definitively displaced? Sacrifice outside that social frame is nothing: a sacrifice performed today and so lacking the mythical structure and tradition in which the meaning of the ritual form of the sacrifice took shape would only be a parody of a sacrifice. It would be what it can under no circumstances be allowed to become, if Bataille's analysis is correct, that is – a thing. Furthermore, the activity of Acéphale was established in a way that served to induce an experience in a way that Bataille later condemned in relation to inner experience.

In the society in which we live today is not the only experience open to us that is analogous to sacrifice that of the massacre, to return to the distinction made by Todorov? This is the only genuine manifestation of the sacrificial impulse, translated into our own social frame. We cannot reconstitute the lost social frame which made actual sacrifice such a significant and consequential act. Certainly such a framework cannot be re-established in a provisional way to make the basis of an enterprise like that of Acéphale meaningful. In order for sacrifice to mean anything its form must be organically present within a particular social structure. It is difficult to see how, in trying to create such a framework through Acéphale, Bataille was doing any more than straining after gnats and that such an activity must ultimately cede place to a sense of the nostalgia for the sacred which he otherwise condemns rather than its reinvigoration. In the process there seems little doubt that Bataille was indeed making of sacrifice a 'thing' and thus expressly destroying its very basis as he perceived it.

In order for sacrifice to have meaning it also requires an object. Yet, to what god could such a sacrifice be made? Although Acéphale was conceived as an anti-Christian association, Bataille was not at all drawn to the idea of blasphemy and the rituals of the black mass. This was something that would have given Christianity too much distinction. He was not, in this sense, a rebel of Christianity, but genuinely sought to go beyond it.

Bataille's idea of sovereignty may be said to take its starting point in the work of the Marquis de Sade, but despite obvious points of contact between them, Bataille's relation with the thought of Sade is far from straightforward. In spite of the fact that both are philosophers of the extreme, and while it has generally been assumed that Bataille's work has a close relation to that of Sade, in fact Bataille was not entirely comfortable with the Divine Marquis and there are elements about Sade that he found disturbing, and in many ways the two men's approaches come from the opposite ends of the spectrum. This is especially the case in relation to the notion of sovereignty.

Bataille and Sade do certainly share a starting point, since both would define sovereignty as an opposition to any form of servility. Bataille expressed what this involved in these terms:

> We cannot reduce ourselves to utility and neither can we negate our condition. That is why we find the *human quality* not in some definite state but in the necessarily undecided battle of the one who refuses *the given*, whatever that may be, providing it is *the given*.[36]

This then is the absolute revolt of surrealism, and it is the point from which all of those drawn to the surrealist position take their departure. From there, however, there is much divergence. For Sade, sovereignty was embodied by a person who had determined his own truth beyond any sense of social responsibility. No limits could be set to his designs since any limit would have meant the curtailment of sovereignty. Above all, one needed to triumph over death in the sense that a genuine sovereignty would not recognise death, but would accept its life as its only reality. As such there would be no death. A sovereign being would simply exist. If he ceased to exist then being would simply come to an end. There could be no experience of death and no anguish at the thought of it. Sade's sovereign man would not acknowledge it at all. There is no relation between life and death: there is only life and non-life. Death, in this sense does not exist.

Sade's position was one of an almost absolute relativism: everything was possible and there were no limits. The universal for him did not exist. One should therefore indulge one's penchants to the full. It was only by such bursting of limits that sovereignty would become possible. Sade denies the notion of otherness and the possibility of communication. In effect, he asserts something like this: 'My only reality is myself and my own desires. I have no responsibility but to follow those desires no matter where they might lead and if they should harm others then one should feel no sense of guilt or contrition.'

In accordance with Sade's uncompromisingly materialist view of the world, if one does evil then it can only be because evil is in one's nature and there is nothing that can be done about it and no reason for us to deny the fact. Sade's philosophy does not justify evil any more than it justifies anything else. It is a profound affirmation of the world in which transcendence and hope are emphatically denied. To this extent Bataille is in accord with Sade. But just as Sade offers an affirmation of the world in an uncontrovertible way, he combines this with an equally emphatic denial of social being. There is for Sade no social truth and no moral standard that should be obeyed. The only truth is what lies within one's own inner being. It is not only society's laws that count for nothing, any boundary placed by life that serves to frustrate one's desire is equally null and void.

The problem raised by Sade's work is where, if we accept this argument, do such desires for sociality emerge from? It must follow from his argument that any desire that arises not from inherent need but from social causes is invalid. Yet in this case, he is thrown back into a pure naturalism in which the life process counts for nothing. There can be no change, no human dynamic; our actions can only be mechanically processed within us at birth. Free will is impossible, since, in so far as it has meaning only in relation to the behaviour of others, then free will requires a social frame in which to function. Sade offers a choice: to be subservient or to be sovereign. Yet his basic postulates mean that there can be no such choice. We must, says Sade, act in accordance with the sovereign nature of the being which nature has imbued us with. But if this sovereignty defines our inner nature, then how can subservience be explained? Doubtless Sade would answer': through socialisation!' But if so, how can social processes, born themselves from human desires, impose such slavery against nature? Nature is either sovereign or it isn't. If it is then such revolt (a revolt to impose servitude!) is impossible. If it isn't then how can Sade say that we should act in accord with its dictates against those that respond to socialisation? It is difficult not to conclude that, despite itself Sade's thought in the end can only legitimate a mechanistic and deterministic fate.

In Sade sovereignty can exist only for oneself. We can recognise others only within the same sovereign realm. Essentially Sade is saying to the world: 'I exist and live in accordance with my own desires. I will never compromise them. I will accept without flinching anything the world may throw at me. Nothing will ever make me bow down and accept conditions that are imposed upon me.'

Bataille accepts this as a preliminary announcement of sovereignty, but it does not satisfy him. We have seen how important socialisation is for Bataille, and it was to bring the notion of sovereignty into the realm of social relations that perhaps represents the most important aspect of his thought.

In essence Sade recognised only personal interests; Bataille was concerned on the other hand with the dissolving of personal interest in a universal generosity. One could not become sovereign if one's interest stopped at oneself. Bataille does start with the individual but he soon recognises an insufficiency. As he denied the social, so Sade denied any idea of communication. Sade's initial insight into sovereignty therefore needs in Bataille's view to be complemented with Hegel's idea of 'recognition'. To be sovereign it is necessary to make the *choice* to live rather than accept the burden of living that is placed above one. Bataille writes: 'Life is whole only when it isn't subordinate to a specific object that exceeds it.'[37]

Like the sacred, sovereignty is something that is expelled from a society that reduces itself to homogeneity. We can still perceive sovereignty as a crucial feature of feudal society, but this sovereignty is destroyed by the bourgeois taste for accumulation. As Bataille writes:

> in the feudal world there was a preference for a *sovereign* use, for an unproductive use, of wealth. The preference of the bourgeois world was reserved, quite on the contrary, for accumulation. The sense of value that predominated in the bourgeoisie caused the richest men to devote their resources to the installation of workshops, factories and mines. The feudal world erected churches, castles, palaces which evoked a sense of wonder.[38]

Medieval society was therefore a society of subjects while bourgeois society becomes a society of things.

Sovereignty is embodied traditionally in the notion of royalty. The king is embodied and entrusted with the sovereignty of the whole society in an objectified and condensed form. But such sovereignty is paradoxically offered, since the king is both esteemed and despised, honoured and abused: he is both the supreme good and the moral danger of a society. Within a society based in the idea of sovereignty, which of course is also heterogeneous in nature, Bataille denies that the systematisation of power relations is present: the king has no power and his sovereignty is directly proportional to his lack of power: if he uses it as a means of power then he abuses sovereignty and transforms himself into a servile being. In fact the sovereignty of the feudal king is largely symbolic, and perceived as such. The issue of sovereignty is the theme of the grail legends before they gained their Christian overlay: the grail represents the quest for a genuine sovereignty that is out of reach of everyday relations.

The recovery of sovereignty within the homogenous society in which we now live lies within the overturning of power relations, something which has been conceptualised in such a devastating way in Hegel's master and slave relation.

For Bataille the apparent sovereignty of the slave is illusory because the process of sovereignty gains its own autonomous will that replaces servitude so that 'the product of his work becomes his master.'[39] Genuine sovereignty therefore requires the renunciation of work. This means that one must live entirely in the present and take no concern for the future.

However, in so far as Bataille identifies work as that activity that provides the key to the human attitude, how can sovereignty take shape through a rejection of work that seems to imply, in Bataille's terms, the denial of our humanness. As we cannot deny the taboo, how can we deny the principle of work? From the same perspective, how can one renounce concern for the future without renouncing life itself? Is it possible, as Bataille advocates, to live entirely in the moment? Is not life always defined by a concern for the next moment? All living creatures are concerned about their own survival, they all strive to push themselves forward. If they do not have any awareness of death, even the most simple organisms are aware of the precariousness of life. And does not awareness of the precariousness of life make it impossible to live without concern for the future? As human beings, the precariousness of life is even more pronounced, since our daily survival as children is ensured only through the care of a whole community of people, who must devote themselves to our welfare against their own immediate concerns. A denial of work and a denial of the needs of the future would imply a denial of the nurturing of children. Without this could the species survive? Bataille himself raises the question without seemingly being aware that it undercuts his argument. He writes: 'If we live sovereignly, the representation of death is impossible, for the present is not subject to the demands of the future.'[40] Yet if this is so is it not a denial of life itself, since Bataille has told us quite categorically that death is the condition of life?

I do not therefore believe that Bataille has found a way around Hegel's dialectic of master and slave with his concept of sovereignty, which remains hanging in the air. For Hegel it is not work that makes one free: it is the experience of work combined with revolt against the condition of work. This is a far more concrete situation that Bataille can maintain with his notion of sovereignty which remains, in the form in which he has argued it, far too confused to be useful. It ignores the fact that it is in the process of revolt the slave becomes transformed: in that process he ceases to be a slave. Even if work represents the means through which he may have gained sovereignty, it is not his end, which is neither work nor the absence of work but a pure state of being. Work in itself is not to be equated with servility. To the contrary, in Bataille's own terms it is the very condition of mankind.

In so far as one recognises the claims for sovereignty, can it ever be other than provisional? Does it not dissolve by being named? Sovereignty perceived as such would become a thing and so would cease to be sovereign. It is like the situation of the king who destroys his sovereignty by assuming power, only to find that in the process the sovereignty he previously embodied has turned to dust. This is a problem that Bataille knows full well, but it doesn't prevent him from advancing his discussion on the basis that it can be named.

Bataille's concept of sovereignty no less retains its validity against the Christian idea of salvation. If we accept salvation, we accept being abandoned to the world and become 'disabled, arrogant marionettes, repelling each other, challenging one another. They claim to love one another, fall into zealous hypocrisy, hence the nostalgia for tempests, for tidal waves.'[41] Work is thus only servile to the extent that it is allowed to stand precisely as a synonym for servility. Sovereignty refuses transcendence and always retains an immanent *raison d'être*: 'every moment lived for its own sake is sovereign'.[42]

Bataille's notion of sovereignty is also based in a rejection of ideas of growth and evolution. Life for him is founded in chance and change takes places on the chemical model of precipitation. There is no gradual evolution towards a set point. Change occurs when a build up of energy reaches the point that it can no longer be contained within its limits and so blossoms, or explodes, into something new. Mankind's own coming was no exception. Bataille implicitly denies the idea that we evolved from monkeys through a process of adaptation. Evolution doubtless played its part, but man's birth was determined by the force of life's desire. It was the pure effusiveness of life that caused our ancestors to emerge on the earth and take up the tools that would give us our specificity as humans and distinguishes us from other animals in the awareness we developed of the dual movement of anguish embodied in life and death and concretised in human eroticism. He expressed this coming into being in a beautiful passage:

> Like skies' lightning, a flash of energy has come time and again to infuse its magic into history's wavering course. Upon various occasions, when hitherto listless, passive and as though asleep, man touched by that electrifying, seemingly heaven-sent passion, has stood suddenly up, clear-eyed and renewed, and has set forth to

conquer; then, the gates of the possible swing wide, as though suddenly waked, he sees within reach what hitherto appeared in dream, only fugitively to his eye. This passing from winter's torpid standstill to springtime's rapid efflorescence seems always to have quickened, men were seized with a dizzying exhilaration which like some strong drink gives a feeling of power. A new life begins: it has lost none of the material harshness which is life's constant, thorny essence, it is no less a perilous struggle, but the fresh possibilities it brings with it have the winy taste of delight.[43]

Mankind did not, therefore, evolve from other animals, but differentiated itself in response to an imperative within us. For Bataille the impulse to change is also a rupture, never a continuity, and mankind came to exist because it desired to exist.

It is in the light of this assumption that we need to foreground Bataille's rejection of the evolution of thought that will reach a summit in absolute knowledge. We are not engaged in a quest for the light of pure reason, and reason does not embody a triumph over the darkness and misunderstanding of mythical thought. This is the background we need to appreciate in order to understand Bataille's focus on rationality.

In the first chapter we mentioned Habermas's critique of Bataille in *The Philosophical Discourse of Modernity* and noted that by reading Bataille through Foucault, Habermas had fundamentally misrepresented the basis of Bataille's work, which he characterised essentially as responding to a project that would aim at the unseating of reason through an investigation of what reason expels and excludes.

There is some truth in such an assertion, but the frame of reference that Habermas established is without doubt alien to Bataille's own concerns. Certainly Bataille did display a hatred of the mind and was very hostile to any form of idealism. It is equally true that his idea of heterology was put forward as a means of examination of what had been excluded from a society that had based itself on the ideology of rationality. However, Bataille was not really concerned with a specific critique of reason, and he would not dispute the dialectic of the Enlightenment. As we have already seen, he does not deny conceptual reason its place in the scheme of things. What he disputes is the exalted claims made on its behalf.

Since Bataille's essential framework denies the gradual evolution of the species, he also denies that reason is a determining feature of mankind's mental make-up. He does not accept that humanity exists on a ladder climbing to that lucidity of reason embodied most perfectly in the absolute of Hegelian philosophy. Rather, reason is an attribute of mankind which responds to nothing in its essence: deprived of reason a man no less remains a man and a man, what's more, whose value *as a man* is not at all diminished by his lack of reason. Conceptual reason is something that has a value in circumstances in which its use is appropriate. However, it is incapable of addressing the real issues of being and is not something on which we can base the idea of mankind. Certainly a man who is deficient in reason is as ill-equipped to deal with life situations which respond to a need for reason as a man who goes on a tiger hunt without being able to shoot. But as a hunter who lacks a gun does not cease to be a hunter if he has other means of confronting his prey, so a man who lacks the basics of conceptual reason may have other means at his disposal that enable him to cope with his mental environment. On the other hand, if a man of reason loses, as a consequence of the very strength of his reasoning, a sense of the inner experience that is appropriate to his life being then he remains a disembodied being: his reason remains trapped in a void, accumulating useless facts and failing to respond to the world in which he lives. Dispensing with reason does not return us to the animal state, nor does it cause us to return to a supposedly 'primitive' state in which we engage in mythical thought. Unreason is itself determined by reason, of which it represents the denied (transgressive) underside. Unreasoning behaviour accentuates our specifically human characteristics appropriate to present day society, bringing the light of reason into relief by comparison. But despite our tendency to call people who act in an unacceptable way 'animals', in fact nothing in such behaviour is ever commensurable with animal behaviour. Rather it is, in Bataille's terms, an example of transgression expressed through the process of its denial.

In this respect, Bataille's own position in relation to the dialectic of enlightenment is much closer to that of Adorno and Horkheimer (and indeed to Habermas himself[44]) than it is to Foucault. There can equally be little doubt that Bataille would be fully in accord with Adorno and Horkheimer in the substance of their critique of the Enlightenment. He would certainly accept the postulate that the Enlightenment presents a dialectic that is double-edged, bringing with it an increase in understanding and systematisation of knowledge on the one hand, but also serving to enhance other forms of domination. While the knowledge brought by the Enlightenment did have the power to unmask social illusions, it also introduced the possibility of new forms of deception. It served to inaugurate the market economy and the notion of calculable gain. In addition it provided a rationalisation for the reification of the universe and brought further proof of our separation from nature. In the words of Adorno and Horkheimer: 'the history of civilisation is the history of the introversions of sacrifice; in other words, the history of renunciation.'[45]

All of this is in fact common to both Adorno and Horkheimer as well as to Bataille, but where they differ is that Adorno and Horkheimer would like to utilise this insight as a means for a deepening of the concept of enlightenment. They do not reject the Enlightenment as a concept but judge it as having failed to measure up to its ambition. As such they accept the ideological claims of the Enlightenment to stand for the light of knowledge against the darkness of myth. At point, this is where Bataille would disagree, since he does not accept the Enlightenment's framework for the distinction between reason and myth.

Bataille accepted that provisional necessity required the Enlightenment to make a stand against mythical thought. However, he insisted on the ideological nature of this movement and did not accept it as a conflict between light and dark. The Enlightenment's claims to have liberated man from the fetters of mythical thought is a hollow one. Conceptual thought itself may have been constrained by mythical thought, but man as a species was not. Any distinction between conceptual reason and mythic reason is technical, and we need to recognise the ideological issues raised by the rise of reason. As Bataille says,

> it was necessary for rationalism to lose the profundity of modes of thought that shackled it. But if we now seek what is possible before us . . . we no longer have any need to construct rational thought, which is effortlessly arranged for us, we are again able to recognise the profound value of the modalities of lost thought.'[46]

This lost mythic domain of thinking has its own value that is comparable to that of conceptual reason. This therefore presents us with a crucial task: how to recover what is vital about mythical, analogical thought.

Bataille would agree with Adorno and Horkheimer when they write: 'the history of civilisation is the history of the introversions of sacrifice; in other words, the history of renunciation'.[47] This confirms Bataille's own perception and ties in with his discussion of the ideological thrust of Christianity. Where Bataille would disagree is on the interpretation they would give to this realisation. Bataille would first of all not accept the break that Adorno and Horkheimer perceive between religion (in its Christian form) and the Enlightenment. He would on the contrary assert that the Enlightenment was the continuation of Christianity in another form, in fact that it was Christianity taken to its highest realisation. The germ of rationalism is contained in Christianity's beginnings. In this sense, if Christianity is a religion, then so is the Enlightenment. Even more, though, Bataille would question Adorno's and Horkheimer's understanding of myth.

For Adorno and Horkheimer, myth is as ideological as reason, if not more so. Indeed, their critique of reason seems to imply that one of the problems of reason is that it has not, as it claimed, divested itself of the ideological function of myth, that is it has not properly *demythologised* itself. As they write: 'Myth turns into enlightenment, and nature into mere objectivity'.[48] For them there is an opposition between reason and myth, and it has been rationality's task to cleanse the mind of the errors of mythical thinking. In this task it has failed and it is not at all, as it is for Bataille, a question of the tyranny of conceptual reason being imposed against mythical thought. For Adorno and Horkheimer, the Enlightenment needs to be continued and rationality must divest itself more rigorously of the conceptions of mythical thought.

For Bataille, however, myth is not ideological since it is a characteristic of a form of society (that is a society founded in heterogeneity) that does not need ideological justification: ideology is necessarily a component of homogeneity. A heterogeneous society, being founded in myth, arises organically from man's inner sensibility. It cannot be imposed externally. In so far as it remains founded in myth it cannot be ideological.

Reason does not replace myth, since it is in its essence itself a myth. It is as it assumes a hegemony over any other mythical forms that it becomes an ideology. This makes of it a thing, and so destroys its mythical structure. It will be recalled that when we discussed Bataille's concepts earlier we explained how an idea like Christianity becomes for Bataille an entity. It is only through gaining an ideological structure, which is asserted through a hegemonic definition, that it becomes analysable in these terms. A myth, in so far as it remains a myth, resists such definition: it cannot become a thing.

Bataille also profoundly disagrees with Adorno and Horkheimer when they consider mythical thinking as a deficient form of reason. This was why they believe it was replaced by reason and their critique of reason is founded in the fact that reason had retained mythical aspects and thus is untrue to itself. Habermas expresses very succinctly what is at stake:

Magical thinking does not allow for basic conceptual distinctions between things and persons, inanimate and animate; between objects that can be manipulated and agents to whom we ascribe actions and linguistic utterances. Only demythologisation dispels this enchantment, which appears to *us* to be a confusion between nature and culture.[49]

For Habermas, as for Adorno and Horkheimer, the attempt by the Enlightenment to master nature was a positive one. The problem was that the process went too far and served not simply to master nature but also served to introduce mastery into human relations, so that we made things of other people. And so Adorno and Horkheimer assert, 'By taking everything unique and individual under its tutelage, it left the uncomprehended whole the freedom, as domination, to strike back at human existence and consciousness by way of things.'[50] What is then required is a more rigorous application of reason. For Bataille this argument is fundamentally flawed since the latter is the inevitable consequence of the attempt to master nature. Furthermore, he refuses the opposition between mythical thinking and reason. The latter does not grow out of the former but must have always been present in man's thinking since the use of tools is unthinkable without the application of reason. Conceptual reason and magical (mythical, analogical) reason are different ways of thinking about the world that are equally valid. Both are present in our beginnings: conceptual reason must have been present for man to be able to use tools; analogical reason served to mediate our ancestor's relation with the cosmos. It was the ideological needs of the Enlightenment that broke down this distinction and inserted the lie that it embodied 'light' against the 'darkness' of myth. From the beginning, in fact, the relation between conceptual and mythical reasoning was analogous to that between taboo and transgression. In the same way, the casting out of mythical reasoning is analogous with the casting out of transgression: conceptual reason, identified with work and the taboo, becomes a supreme good. It is thus a feature of homogeneity. Yet in reality neither conceptual reason nor mythical reason define our nature as human beings; both are attributes for enabling us to come to terms with the nature of our existence.

Belonging to the surrealist generation, Bataille's concern was far more with the re-integration of mythical thinking into Western discourse, than with undermining reason with its 'other' and it was certainly the last thing on Bataille's mind to criticise reason by means of a 'rhetorically affirmed other of reason'[51], as Habermas contends. Bataille despised rhetoric as much as he distrusted the mind, and his distrust of the latter was a rejection of idealism, not reason. By positing the idea of an acephalic, headless figure, or with the suggestion of a science of heterology, Bataille was not putting forward a critique that was specifically of reason except, perhaps, in so far as reason could be equated with utility.

For Bataille it is not reason but interdiction that is the essence of mankind. If we can lose our reason without ceasing to be human, we cannot lose our sense of interdiction without at the same time losing our being as humans. Our whole definition is tied up with taboo and a sense of prohibitions. Despite Christianity's attempt to foist guilt onto the individual, the nature of collective guilt remains at the heart of our definition of ourselves as a species and the issues this raises need to be confronted if we are to rebuild a sense of collective values. Bataille's own attempts to explore this through group activity may seem misguided, but there is no denying the vital needs to which such activity responded. Reason is unable to provide a satisfactory framework for such a revision of values since reason is in complicity with the denial of the collective through having sought to unseat mythical reasoning and the idea of the sacred. Reason also serves the servility of things. At the same time it is quite unable to give an adequate replacement for the lack of the sacred in anything that touches our innermost being and provides a genuine rationale for living. Its basis can only reinforce our sense of alienation from the world. As Bataille put it:

> There is in nature and there subsists in man a movement which exceeds the bounds, that can never be anything but partially reduced to order. We are generally unable to grasp it. Indeed it is by definition that which can never be grasped, but we are conscious of being in its power: the universe that bears us along answers no purpose that reason defines, and if we try to make it answer to God, all we are doing is associating irrationally the infinite excess in the presence of which our reason exists with our reason itself.[52]

For Bataille, then, our primary need is to re-invent a sense of community embodied in a new conception of the sacred that responds to our contemporary needs. Living needs to be based on the experience of the world, not in abstract concepts. Ideological notions, from Christianity to reason, represent a poverty of experience against which we can do no more than measure the emptiness of our lives. We need, therefore, to re-invent myth.

Bataille's work in this area nevertheless begs the question of whether the creation of a social myth is possible in such a complex society as we inhabit today. We have to wonder if homogeneity is not the price we have to pay for the complexity and diversity of a modern society that is founded on the possibilities raised by individual choice. Any re-invigoration of collective values must pass through the individual and retain the idea of individual choice. Is this a feasible project? If we pay attention to the essential issues raised by Bataille's investigation, we will see that he asserts that there is a paradox between the fact that the freedom so vaunted by contemporary society (of speech, association and choice) is the hallmark of the social homogeneity that deprives the concepts of freedom of any real and effective meaning. In homogeneous society, diversity of opinion and individual freedom of choice serve the role that transgression once served in heterogeneous society, but now reinforces a repressive order of things. How, in such conditions, can the possibilities of heterogeneous society be re-opened? Would not any potential social myth run up against the brick wall of individualism? Can it even be possible to reconcile Bataille's idea of sovereignty (refusing what is given purely because it is given) with a social myth shared by all?

Bataille was fully aware of these difficulties, and yet he nevertheless persisted in believing that the attempt to repair social solidarity was essential and revealed a path that had to be explored if we were to confront our real condition in the world and recover a sense of elemental harmony. He perceived the possible germ of such solidarity in the efforts of the surrealists to re-invigorate the idea of myth and analogy in an appropriate social context, but had to recognise that surrealism had done no more than take a very small first step in this direction. He saw a stronger affirmation in the possibilities of communism, but the collapse of communism and its woeful failure to establish any founding myth in which people could believe in a meaningful way is one of the great failures of the age.

But if social solidarity was once founded in a sense of collective guilt in the primal crime that separated us from our roots in nature, can a joyful embrace of guilt – such as Bataille experienced through his inner experience – provide the possibility for a re-invigoration of society? How can individualism be transformed back into social belonging? These are the issues Bataille tried to tackle in such a moving way. To say that he was unable to answer them is hardly to diminish his work, but on the contrary reveals how important it remains.

Bataille's work is at once central to our times and yet curiously distanced from it. The concomitant exigencies of much of European discourse in the twentieth century – despair and engagement – passed him by. If his work engages in an uncompromising way with anguish, we should not allow this to blind us to the fact that Bataille's endeavour was overwhelmingly affirmative: to the end he remained determined to say 'yes' to the universe no matter what it offered. The world and the place he assigns us as human beings within it may be disturbing but Bataille nevertheless refuses to surrender to cynicism, something he considered complacent.

Adorno asked if there could be poetry after Auschwitz. It was a question that Bataille would undoubtedly have dismissed as naive and reply that Auschwitz had made poetry more than ever essential. But for Bataille, also, it was false to see Auschwitz as representing any watershed in mankind's history. Bataille's whole thinking assumes that the enormity of what happened in the concentration camps was not an aberration of mankind, rather it showed the danger we run if we engage in a collective repression of our fundamental internal violence. We can only be surprised at the degradation represented by the concentration camps if we have allowed ourselves to be deceived by the project of the Enlightenment. Far from there being any doubt about whether poetry might be possible after Auschwitz, poetry was the only possible response, since poetry alone for Bataille contains within it the germ for a re-figuration of the sacred which he saw as being the necessary task for the integration of transgressive violence back into social being and make possible a genuinely human society.

This is the affirmative kernel of Bataille's thinking. For all the lacunae and inconsistencies his thinking reveals, Bataille is a writer of unquestionable authenticity and among those who have believed the 'truth in one mind and one body' demanded by Rimbaud was possible.

When he was planning to found a literary movement with Michel Leiris and Theodore Fraenkel way back in the twenties, he wanted to found the principle as one of an unconditional 'yes' to the universe. Throughout his life Bataille remained true to this essential affirmation.

Yet, as with everything else in Bataille, this affirmation was paradoxical, since it relied on an essential refusal of any form of servitude. The 'yes' offered to the universe therefore resided on a substratum of refusal. Both this refusal and this affirmation nevertheless respond to an essential invigoration of life. In this sense we might compare Bataille's work with that of a man who experienced in a direct way the horrors of our age. I am thinking here of Victor Serge, whose life was a confrontation of the violence at the heart of being. Yet Serge always remained affirmative, always insisting that what we needed to do was 'get into the habit of living'. Bataille, one feels, could not have expressed what he felt was the essential task of life any better.

Suggestions for further reading

The reader who wishes to take an interest in Bataille further is well advised to start with Bataille's own writings. His most important work is now available in generally excellent translations. One would be well advised to take *Eroticism* as a starting point, since it is clearly written and gives a summation of Bataille's overall themes. The texts of *The Tears of Eros* and *Prehistoric Art* provide supplementary arguments on Bataille's ideas of taboo and eroticism and both are splendidly illustrated, the latter including what are perhaps the finest photographs we have of the Lascaux caves. The first volume of *The Accursed Share* is essential for an understanding of the notion of the general economy. Volumes two and three (in English collected together in one volume) are patchy and the argument is more confused. Volume two, *The History of Eroticism* presents, in a different focus, the basis of the argument developed in *Eroticism*. The third volume, *Sovereignty*, is one of Bataille's weaker books. *Theory of Religion*, connected to the same debate, is an important book but is one of Bataille's most difficult works and is therefore not recommended as introductory reading. As providing a general overview of Bataille's work during the inter-war period, *Visions of Excess*, and *Writings on Laughter, Sacrifice, Nietzsche, Un-Knowing*, an issue of the journal *October*, can hardly be bettered, both being well-chosen selections and highly recommended (the latter work also includes excellent essays by Annette Michelson and Allen S. Weiss, which are among the best texts written in English on Bataille). *The Absence of Myth* collects together Bataille's writings on surrealism. These mostly date from after the Second World War and so both complement the other two anthologies as well as providing important background reading into his later thought. For those most interested in the subjective aspects of Bataille's thought, it is perhaps best to begin with *Guilty* and *On Nietzsche*, both of which are available in excellent translations. *Inner Experience*, although its publication preceeds that of *Guilty* and *On Nietzsche* and is the more important book, is a less accessible text whose English translation is unfortunately awkward and difficult to read, having the feel of a first draft rather than a finalised translation. The novels offer a different point of access into his world. Both *The Story of the Eye* and *Blue of Noon* are excellent translations that capture the transgressive sense of Bataille's ideas. The former is Bataille's first book and contains a powerful emotional charge, with its content very much embedded in Bataille's experiences of adolescence (when, we should remember, he was very serious and devout). The emotional charge is equally strong in *Blue of Noon*, written in the wake of the break-up of Bataille's first marriage and haunted by the rise of fascism. *The Impossible*, which is halfway between being a novel and a philosophical text, is a very strange book indeed. The most devastating of the novels, though, is *Madame Edwarda*, which, despite it brevity, is one of the most disturbing novels ever written. The currently available English edition does now include Bataille's preface, as well as a fascinating article by Yukio Mishima, as well as other disturbing erotic tales, *My Mother* and *The Dead Man*. *L'Abbé C.* is perhaps the closest Bataille came to writing a conventional novel in so far as he attempts to make a clear delineation of character and it is a tale of betrayal and faith set during the Second World War.

Serious students of Bataille's work need to engage with it in its totality, since Bataille hated the idea of completion or closure and his fragments and rambling ruminations are often as important as his more coherently developed work. One should therefore try to consult his *Oeuvres complètes*, of which there are now twelve volumes (Paris: Gallimard) (1971 to date).

Notes

PREFACE

1 Quoted in Bataille, *The Accursed Share* Vol. 2 (*Sovereignty*) p. 381.
2 *Inner Experience* p. 199.

1 INTRODUCTION

1 In fact it had previously been translated in 1968, but seems to have had little impact.
2 It was at the International Cultural Centre held at Cérisy-la-Salle between 29 and 9 July 1972 (devoted to him and to Artaud) that Bataille was consecrated as the patron saint of post-structuralism. Philippe Sollers, Roland Barthes, Denis Hollier, Marceline Pleynet, Jean-Louis Houdebine and Julia Kristeva were among those who gave papers. Derrida's essay on Bataille, 'From restricted to general economy: a Hegelianism without reserve' is included in *Writing and Difference* (translated by Alan Bass), 1978, London: Routledge & Kegan Paul. Foucault's 'Préface à la transgression' was originally published in *Critique* nos 195–6 (1962) and was included in Michel Foucault, *Language, Counter-Memory, Practice; Selected Essays and Interviews* (translated by Donald F. Bouchard and Sherry Simon), 1977, Oxford: Basil Blackwell. The same issue of *Critique* also included other articles by Barthes and Sollers.
3 Foucault, 'Préface à la transgression' op. cit.
4 ibid., p. 33.
5 We need to appreciate here that in the 1920s there was a feeling that the French philosophical tradition that had culminated in Bergson had reached a dead-end. What revitalised it was the incorporation of German philosophy, most especially Hegel, who was hardly known in France prior to 1920. The electrifying lectures of Alexandre Kojève, and the work of Alexandre Koyré, Jean Hypollite and Jean Wahl served to make Hegelianism central to French thought, to the extent that even thinkers like Merleau-Ponty, Sartre and Camus, who were temperamentally not drawn to Hegelian conceptualisation, nevertheless needed to come to terms with it. Bataille belonged to the generation who were under the sway of Hegel and he was certainly no exception to this general influence.

6 Quoted by Barry Smart in *Michel Foucault* 1985, London: Routledge, p. 141.

7 Jürgen Habermas, 'Between eroticism and general economics: Georges Bataille' in *The Philosophical Discourse of Modernity* (translated by Frederick Lawrence) 1987, Oxford: Polity Press.

8 Hollier, *Against Architecture* p. 23.

9 ibid., p. 25.

10 See *The Accursed Share* Part 3 (*Sovereignty*) (the essays 'Nietzsche and Jesus' and 'Nietzsche and the Transgression of Prohibition').

11 ibid., p. 380.

12 'Un-knowing, and its consequences' in *Writings on Laughter, Sacrifice, Nietzsche, Unknowing* p. 81.

13 J.G. Merquior, *From Prague to Paris* 1986, London: Verso, p. 113.

14 *Inner Experience* p. 13.

15 *Sovereignty* p. 341.

2 LIFE AND CONTEXT OF WORK

1 Preface to *Literature and Evil*.

2 'Autobiographical Note' in *Writings On Laughter, Sacrifice, Nietzsche, Unknowing* p. 107.

3 ibid., p. 110.

3 THEMES AND INTELLECTUAL BACKGROUND

1 He expressed this very clearly: 'To shrink from fundamental stability isn't less cowardly than to hesitate about shattering it. Perpetual instability is more boring that adhering strictly to a rule.' *Guilty* p. 28–9.

2 *Eroticism* p. 274.

3 'Sociology and the Relationships Between "Society", "Organism" and "Being"', in Denis Hollier (ed.), *The College of Sociology 1937–1939* p. 74.

4 Originally published in 1937, it was re-issued in 1977 (Paris: Sagittaire).

5 ibid., p. 80.

6 Marx, 'Economic and philosophical manuscripts' in *Early Writings* (translated by Rodney Livingstone and Gregor Benton) 1975, Harmondsworth: Penguin, p. 350.

7 Only one of Chestov's books seems currently available in English: *Speculation and Revelation* (translated by Richard Martin) 1982, Athens: Ohio University Press; *Athens and Jerusalem* was translated (again by Richard Martin) in 1966, Athens: Ohio University Press. Other works were published during his lifetime: *Penultimate Words* in 1916; *All Things Are Possible* (translated by S.S. Koteliansky) in 1920; *In Job's Balances* (translated by Camilla Coventry and C.A. Macarthnay) in 1932.

8 In collaboration with Teresa Beresovski-Chestov, Bataille translated Chestov's book, *L'idée du bien chez Tolstoï et Nietzsche*, published in 1926. This book appears never to have been translated into English.

9 *Inner Experience* p. 109.

10 'Unknowing: laughter and tears' in *Writings On Laughter, Sacrifice,*

Nietzsche, Un-Knowing p. 96.
11 *On Nietzsche* p. 55.
12 Sarane Alexandrian, 'Georges Bataille ou l'amour noir' in *Les Libérateurs de l'amour* 1977, Paris: Seuil p. 259.
13 'The Alleluia, catechism of Dianus' in *Guilty* p. 158.

4 TOWARDS A SOCIOLOGY OF ABUNDANCE

1 *Inner Experience* p. 219.
2 Note included in *La Révolution surréaliste*, no. 2, 15th January 1925, p. 31.
3 *La Révolution surréaliste*, no. 1, 1 December 1924, p. 2.
4 See Elisabeth Roudinesco's *Jacques Lacan & Co: a History of Psycho-analysis in France* Vol. 2 (1925–1985) 1990, London: Free Associations.
5 In a note in the daybook of the Bureau of Surrealist Research, a note assigns to Pierre Naville the task of collecting information about courses in sociology and the study of languages and religion in order for a critique to be made of it, but this does not appear to have been pursued.
6 Published in Bataille, *The Absence of Myth* 1994 (forthcoming), London: Verso.
7 Michel Foucault, *The Order of Things: an Archaeology of the Human Sciences* 1973, New York: Vintage Books p. 387.
8 André Breton, 'Second manifeste du surréalisme' in *Oeuvres complètes* Vol. 1, 1988, Paris: Gallimard p. 782.
9 'Surrealism and how it differs from existentialism' in *The Absence of Myth*.
10 'War and the philosophy of the sacred' in *The Absence of Myth*.
11 ibid.
12 *Documents* has recently been re-published in facsimile by Jean-Michel Place (1992 – 2 volumes).
13 This at least is what we have generally been led to believe. Both Leiris and Bataille intimated that Carl Einstein was a conventional art historian who had little real involvement. This, however, is far from the truth – Einstein was a fascinating figure, and his writings have recently been published. See Carl Einstein, *Ethnologie de l'art moderne* 1993, Paris: André Dimanche.
14 The publication was also properly funded, unlike *La Révolution surréaliste*, which had no benefactor but was funded by the surrealists themselves.
15 'Formless' in *Visions of Excess* p. 31.
16 In fact this is characteristic of surrealist journals in general, which always maintained a wide range of intellectual enquiry without ever degenerating into eclecticism. *Documents* nevertheless had the widest range of all surrealist journals and was the only one that gave such a high profile to current scholarly work.
17 Leiris, 'From the impossible Bataille to the impossible *Documents*' in *Brisées: Broken Branches* (translated by Lydia Davis) 1989, San Francisco: West Point Press, p. 241.
18 Quoted in ibid., p. 242.
19 Bataille, 'Base materialism and gnosticism' in *Visions of Excess* p. 51.
20 Marina Galetti, 'Masses, a failed collège?' 1989, *Stanford French Review* XII(1).

21 We are indebted to Denis Hollier for a superbly edited collection of documents relating to the College, which enables us to have some precision about its activities, even if he has unfortunately seen fit to accompany it with redundant and typically tendentious commentary. See Dennis Hollier (ed.) *The College of Sociology 1937–1939*.

22 Denis Hollier, (ed.) *The College of Sociology 1937–39* p. 5.

23 ibid., p. 5.

24 Between them they gave fourteen lectures; the other presentations were by Michel Leiris, Alexandre Kojève, René M. Guastella, Anatole Lewitsky, Hans Meyer, Jean Paulhan and Georges Duthuit, who each gave one apiece, and Pierre Klossowski, who gave two (one in collaboration with Denis de Rougemont).

25 Bataille, 'The College of Sociology' in ibid., p. 336.

26 ibid., p. 334.

27 Michel Fardoulis-Lagrange, *G.B. ou un ami présomptueux* 1968, Paris: Le Soleil Noir, p. 81.

28 ibid., p. 72–3.

29 See 'Vers un nouveau myth? Prémonitions et défiances' in *VVV* no. 4, February 1944. This letter is also included in Patrick Waldberg/Isabelle Waldberg, *Un Amour Acéphale: Correspondence 1940–49* edited by Michel Waldberg (Paris: La Difference, 1992) where the context surrounding its publication is explained.

30 Bataille, *On Nietzsche* p. xxvii.

31 *Méthode de méditation* in *Oeuvres complètes* Vol. 6 p. 215.

32 ibid.

33 Bataille, *Inner Experience* p. 81.

34 *Inner Experience* p. 7.

35 It seems that originally Bataille had wanted to co-edit it with Roger Caillois, but the latter objected to the limitation to books. Instead Caillois formed his own, equally brilliant, review *Diogenes*, which presents a fascinating complement to *Critique* and which likewise is still being published today.

36 Even *L'Abbé C* can be seen to respond to a sense of dissemblance, being presented as a narrative written by 'Charles C', with notes by 'Chianne', and introduced by an editor. The use of different narrative voices is of course a common strategy of novelists, but in Bataille this does not seem to respond to any perceived structural necessity but from a need to dissemble and distance himself from the narrative voice. Similarly in *The Impossible*, which is half way between a novel and a theoretical text, the main narrative section, 'A Story of Rats' is presented as the journal of 'Dianus', while the section entitled 'Dianus' is 'drawn from the Notebooks of Monsignor Alpha'.

37 *Madame Edwarda* is particularly interesting. Originally published in 1941, it carries a publication date of 1937 and the name of a small publisher, Solitaire; it was re-published in 1945; this edition was dated 1942. A third edition was published more openly by Jean-Jacques Pauvert in 1956, still under the pseudonym of Pierre Angélique but this time including an introduction by Georges Bataille! *Le Mort* was not in fact published during his lifetime, but would have appeared under the name of Pierre Angélique if it had been. *WC*, his first novel, which he destroyed, was to have been

published under the name 'Tropmann', who became the main character in *Blue of Noon*.

38 See Jules Monnerot, 'Sur Georges Bataille' in *Inquisitions* 1974, Paris: José Corti, p. 216.

39 *On Nietzsche* p. 68.

40 'The Pornographic Imagination' in *The Story of the Eye* p. 105.

41 One might express a little surprise that Bataille gave evidence for the defence at the trial of Jean-Jacques Pauvert over publication of the works of Sade in 1955. His evidence, which is published in *Oeuvres complètes* Vol. 12, p. 455, will certainly surprise those who regard him purely as being concerned with excess as a value in itself. He fully agrees that there are aspects of Sade's books that could encourage voyeurs of death and suffering and therefore they should not be freely available. He states that as a librarian he would not allow free access to them: anyone who wishes to consult them must obtain authorisation. Nevertheless he states 'I consider that for someone who wants to go to the bottom of what it means to be man, the reading of Sade is not only desirable, but absolutely necessary.' As such Sade's books are analogous to medical textbooks and he defends Pauvert's edition precisely because it is expensive and therefore unlikely to come into undesirable hands. These comments are, I think, consistent with what Bataille generally believed.

42 *L'Abbé C.* p. 101.

43 *Guilty* p. 113.

44 'Unknowing and rebellion' in *Writings On Laughter, Sacrifice, Nietzsche, Unknowing* p. 86.

45 *Inner Experience* p. 92.

46 *Eroticism* p. 33.

5 EXPENDITURE AND THE GENERAL ECONOMY

1 Bataille, *The Accursed Share* p. 12.

2 *The Accursed Share* p. 20.

3 It is translated in *Visions of Excess* pp. 116–29.

4 ibid., p. 117.

5 Marcel Mauss, *The Gift* (translated by Ian Cunnison) 1966, London: Routledge & Kegan Paul.

6 *The Accursed Share* Vol. 2 (*Sovereignty*) p. 351.

7 For recent accounts of the basis of Aztec sacrifice see Olga Clardinnen, *The Aztecs* 1991, Cambridge: Cambridge University Press; and Christian Duverger, *La Fleur létale: économie du sacrifice aztèque* 1979, Paris: Seuil.

8 Duverger, op. cit., p. 233.

9 Bataille, *Theory of Religion* p. 49.

10 Tzvetan Todorov, *The Conquest of America* (translated by Richard Howard), 1984: New York: Harper & Row.

11 ibid., p. 144.

12 ibid., p. 145.

13 Bataille, *The Accursed Share* p. 171.

14 ibid., p. 174.

15 ibid., p. 174.
16 ibid., p. 171.
17 ibid., p. 172.
18 See Norman O. Brown, *Life Against Death: The Psychoanalytical Meaning of History* 1959, Middletown, Connecticut: Wesleyan University Press.
19 ibid., p. 265.
20 ibid.
21 ibid., p. 170.
22 Marx, *Economic and Philosophical Manuscripts* pp. 328–30.
23 *The Accursed Share* p. 36.
24 Quoted in Istvan Mészáros, *Marx's Theory of Alienation*, 1970, London: Merlin Press, p. 269.
25 'L'économie à la mesure de l'univers' in *Oeuvres complètes* VII p. 15.
26 *The Accursed Share* Vol. 1 p. 11.

6 DEATH, COMMUNICATION AND THE EXPERIENCE OF LIMITS

1 In fact, Bataille devoted three books to eroticism, emphasising the importance he attached to it. The first, *The History of Eroticism* was written in around 1950 as the second part of *The Accursed Share*, but was only published posthumously. It provided him with a basic framework but the argument developed is substantially different in *Eroticism*. The third, *The Tears of Eros*, can be considered as a supplement to *Eroticism* dealing with the visual arts.
2 Bataille, *Inner Experience* p. 89.
3 *The Accursed Share* Vol. 2 (*The History of Eroticism*) p. 84.
4 ibid., p. 11.
5 Bataille, *Eroticism* p. 29.
6 ibid., p. 86.
7 ibid., p. 63.
8 ibid., p. 59.
9 ibid., p. 241.
10 Bataille, 'Explication de mes écrits' in *Oeuvres complètes* Vol. 7, 1988, Paris: Gallimard, p. 527.
11 Bataille, *Theory of Religion*, p. 74–5.
12 We should here make it clear that when Bataille speaks about 'perverse' sexual behaviour, the word is used in a sense opposed to the 'naturalness' of reproductive sexuality. He does not consider 'perversion' in the sense in which it is generally understood today, i.e. in terms of deviation from the norms of sexual activity. In actual fact, Bataille seems to have been largely uninterested in the mechanics of the sexual act itself. What we actually do is of little interest to him: it is the psychic mechanism involved in how we act that concerns him. Bataille is not at all an advocate of polymorphous sexuality or of exploring the physical potential of our bodies any more than he is an advocate of sexual liberation. For him these are secondary problems of little real interest. His area of interest is almost exclusively the existential frame of sexual activity.

13 Bataille, *Theory of Religion* p. 124.
14 ibid., p. 128.
15 Bataille, 'L'Érotisme et la fascination de la mort', conference given 12 February 1957, Le Nef de Paris Editions, p. 3. This is discussed, in a slightly different form in *Eroticism*.
16 *Eroticism* p. 90.
17 ibid., p. 91.
18 *La Critique sociale* was reissued in facsimile in 1983 with an introduction by Souvarine which emphasises the importance of Colette Peignot to the journal. Souvarine's introduction includes libellous comments about Bataille (suggesting, without offering the slightest shred of evidence, that he was a fascist sympathiser), the tone of which makes it clear that he still felt bitter and jealous about Bataille even after fifty years.
19 These articles are reproduced in Laure, *Écrits rétrouvés*, 1987, Paris: Les Cahiers des Brisants.
20 His emotional turmoil is recounted in *Blue of Noon* in which different commentators have suggested that the characters of Dirty or Xenie are based on Laure. There may be some truth in this, although as Bataille barely knew Laure when he wrote this novel we should treat any such contention with a great deal of caution. Michel Surya, in his biography of Bataille, *Georges Bataille, La mort à l'oeuvre* (1987) Paris: Garamont, disputes that either character can be likened to Laure and perhaps he is right.
21 To the extent that he was unable really to write anything about her: whenever he tried to, anguish would overcome him and he left unfinished the *Life of Laure* he had wanted to write. In many ways, one might say that Bataille experienced Laure's death as a sacrifice – it affected the depths of his being in a way that made the experiences of Acéphale anodyne.
22 This was a conference given at the College of Sociology and is published in the translation of Denis Hollier's *The College of Sociology 1937–1939* pp. 24–32.
23 *Écrits de Laure* 1985, Paris: Jean-Jacques Pauvert, p. 85.
24 *On Nietzsche* p. 21.
25 *Écrits de Laure*. p. 89.
26 'Vie de Laure' in ibid., p. 281.
27 *Inner Experience* p. 126.
28 *On Nietzsche* p. 149.
29 *Guilty* p. 29.
30 For some reflection on this question see the responses to a questionnaire that asked 'Why do you not believe in God?'
31 *Guilty* p. 85.
32 *Guilty* p. 23.
33 Duthuit, et al., 'Vers un nouveau mythe?' *op. cit.*
34 It may be that our psychology has retained an element of the sense of sacrifice in individual terms, and that this can be experienced in eroticism: in this respect Bataille is more convincing.
35 *On Nietzsche* p. 57.
36 *The Accursed Share* Vol. 2 (*Sovereignty*), p. 343.
37 *On Nietzsche* p. xxvii.
38 *The Accursed Share* Vol. 2 p. 240.

39 *Inner Experience* p. 129.
40 ibid., p. 219.
41 *Inner Experience* p. 129.
42 *The Accursed Share* Vol. 2, p. 285.
43 *Prehistoric Art: The Birth of Painting* p. 22.
44 We might here point out in passing the possible correspondences between Bataille's idea of 'communication' and Habermas's of 'communicative action'.
45 *The Dialectic of Enlightenment* p. 71.
46 'Surrealism and How it Differs from Existentialism' in *The Absence of Myth*.
47 Theodor Adorno and Max Horkheimer, *The Dialectic of Enlightenment* (translated by John Cumming) 1979, London: Verso, p. 71.
48 *The Dialectic of Enlightenment* p. 99.
49 *The Philosophical Discourse of Modernity* p. 115.
50 *The Dialectic of Enlightenment* p. 41.
51 Habermas, op. cit.
52 *Eroticism* p. 40.

Bibliography

TRANSLATIONS:

Manet (translated by Austryn Wainhouse and James Emmons), 1955, Geneva: Skira, London: Macmillan.

Prehistoric Painting: Lascaux or the Birth of Art (translated by Austryn Wainhouse), 1955, Geneva: Skira; London: Macmillan;

Eroticism (translated by Mary Dalwood) 1962, London: Calder & Boyas, re-issued 1987, San Fransisco: City Lights, London: Marian Boyars.

Literature and Evil (translated by Alastair Hamilton), 1973, London: Calder & Boyars.

Visions of Excess: Selected Writings 1927–1939 (translated by Allan Stoekl), 1985, Manchester: Manchester University Press.

Writings on Laughter, Sacrifice, Nietzsche, Un-Knowing (translated by Annette Michelson), *October* no. 36, Spring 1986.

Inner Experience (translated by Leslie Anne Boldt), 1988, Albany: State University.

Guilty (translated by Bruce Boone), 1988, Venice, California: Lapis Press.

The Accursed Share (translated by Robert Hurley), 1988, New York: Zone Books.

Theory of Religion (translated by Robert Hurley), 1988, New York: Zone Books.

The Tears of Eros (translated by Peter Connor), 1989, San Fransisco: City Lights.

The Impossible (translated by Robert Hurley), 1991, San Fransisco: City Lights.

The Trial of Gilles de Rais (translated by Robert Robinson), 1991: Los Angeles: Amok.

On Nietzsche (translated by Bruce Boone), 1992, London: Athlone Press.

The Absence of Myth (translated by Michael Richardson), 1994, London: Verso.

See also:

Denis Hollier (ed) *The College of Sociology (1937–39)* (translated by Betsy Wing), 1988, Minneapolis: University of Minnesota Press.

Narratives:

The Beast At Heaven's Gate (Madame Edwarda) (translated by Austryn Wainhouse), 1956, Paris: Olympia Press.

My Mother (translated by Austryn Wainhouse), 1972, London: Jonathan Cape.

The Story of the Eye (translated by Joachim Neugroschel), 1977, New York: Urizen Books; 1979, London: Marion Boyers; 1982, Harmondsworth: Penguin.

Blue of Noon (translated by Harry Matthews), 1979 London: Marion Boyars.

L'Abbé C (translated by Philip A. Facey), 1983, London: Marion Boyars.

My Mother, Madame Edwarda, The Dead Man (translated by Austryn Wainhouse), 1989, London: Marion Boyars.

SECONDARY SOURCES:

Hollier, Denis, *Beyond Architecture* (translated by Betsy Wing), 1990, Cambridge: MIT

Land, Nick, *The Taste for Annihilation: Georges Bataille and Violent Nihilism*, 1992, London: Routledge.

Libertson, Joseph, *Proximity: Levinas, Blanchot, Bataille and Communication*, 1982, The Hague: Martinus Nihoff.

Pefanis, Julian, *Heterology and the Postmodern: Bataille, Baudrillard, Lyotard*, 1991, Durham & London: Duke University Press.

Richman, Michèle, *Beyond the Gift: Reading Georges Bataille*, 1982, Baltimore: Johns Hopkins.

Shaviro, Steven, *Passion and Excess: Blanchot, Bataille, and Literary Theory*, 1990, Tallahassee: Florida State University Press.

special issue of *Yale French Studies*, no. 78 (1990)

Articles:

Calas, Nicolas, 'Acephalic mysticism' in *Hemispheres* II no. 6 (1945), reprinted in *Transfigurations: Art Critical Essays in the Modern Period* 1985, Ann Arbour: UMI Research Press.

Habermas, Jürgen, 'Between eroticism and general economics: Georges Bataille' in *The Philosophical Discourse of Modernity* (translated by Frederick Lawrence), 1987, Oxford: Polity Press.

Michelson, Annette, 'Heterology and the critique of instrumental reason', 1986, *October* 36.

Sontag, Susan, 'The pornographic imagination' first published in *Styles of Radical Will*, 1967, London: Martin Secker & Warburg

Weiss, Allen S., 'Impossible sovereignty: between *The Will to Power* and *The Will to Chance*' 1986, *October* 36.

Name index

Subject index